PRA
RAYMOND
POTEET

"When I was first approached by Dr. Dick Dijkman about the IBC process, I told him my negative experience with "whole" life insurance right out of dental school. It was an experience that I would never want to repeat again in my life. All I could think of was that "whole" life insurance was money down the "hole". But, I kept an open mind and thought, why not read the book, "Becoming your own banker". What did I have to lose? After reading the book several times, I was confused but became fascinated with the potential of this system of infinite banking. I contemplated, could this be true or is it some type of scam. I was still skeptical because I am single and have no children. So why did I need so much life insurance. Who will I pass this on to? I was even more frightened that I would have to overfund this policy with so much money. Then I met Ray Poteet during a seminar, and everything started to make sense. With Mr. Poteet's coaching and explaining the power of the infinite banking concept, I felt invigorated to now have a future of financing everything for myself and my business. But I wasn't satisfied until I did more of my own research and understanding of the process. Then I took a leap of faith and was onto my first dividend paying whole life policy. I was amazed how easy it was to take a loan from my cash value in 30 days to loan my business. Since then, I have paid off over $500,000 to 3rd party lenders through the IBC process and recaptured the interest back to me.

I currently have 2 life insurance policies and starting on my 3rd. I really appreciate the one on one help offered by Ray Poteet and his team and having an awesome study club meeting for mentoring. I now have been banking for the last 5+ years and can honestly say that this system of financing and building wealth works! But you have to invest into the time it takes to learn and understand the process. It's no different than learning to ride a bicycle for the first time."

Randy L. Mow, DDS www.drmowdds.com

"We have been working with Ray Poteet and Dr. Dick Dijkman for several years. It was Dr. Dijkman who first introduced us to the Infinite Banking Concept. It is working well for us. It gives us hope and certainty in an ever-changing world. We are excited about the opportunities that now present themselves for a multigenerational family organization that can serve the financial needs of ourselves, our children and grandchildren.

We have found both these gentlemen to be extremely helpful and patient in helping get us started on our journey towards becoming infinite bankers. They are men of integrity who clearly see that their financial well-being is tied inextricably to your success. They make themselves extremely available if you have concerns or questions. Our son even called Ray regarding some beginners' questions he had and was astounded to learn that Ray was on vacation in Hawaii, yet, his call was returned within minutes of its placement!! It is hard to find such a willingness to help and serve in our modern world. We HIGHLY recommend the IBC plan and implore you to listen to what they have to say. It will change your life."

-- Eric Heap, D.D.S & Patricia Taylor
www.zdentist.com

Private Family Financing is the most important financial information I have ever learned. PFF is the information I have been searching for all my life. It is the TRUTH. It is a rock solid strategy that allows me to sleep at night knowing I no longer have to concern myself with the stock market or economy. I no longer have to take unnecessary risks with my money where I am not in control. I am able to keep the promises I made to my family and I know in my heart that my wife and child will have a better quality of life. Ray Poteet is the smartest business man I know. I don't do anything in business without seeking Ray's advice first. Ray is my mentor and friend and tremendous example of the kind of man I strive to be... a man who will leave a legacy.

Dr. David Pietsch

When I first met Ray 8 years ago I practiced the "buy with cash whenever possible" and "buy term life insurance and invest the difference" approach to my family finances. I was in my late 50's and thought I had done well for my family. Ray totally changed this belief for me and has helped me change my ways, my family's ways, and countless other families' ways.

I initially started my Private Family Financing (PFF) system to take over my home mortgage since I didn't have any other debts. The original plan was for this to take about 4 to 5 years on my recently refinanced 15-year mortgage. However, once I understood what was going on and how I could move resources that I had just sitting, I added to my PFF system and was able to take over my mortgage completely within the first 18 months and keep those dollars that were going outside the family to stay and grow within the family.

Another key change in my finances was being able to move my Tax Sheltered Annuity money that was in the market at a time when the market was falling significantly. Immediately I recovered all the loss of value just with the initial death benefit to the family and I got to use that money at the same time. This fact was a huge relief to me. That value has continued to grow without the concern of market fluctuations or taxes.

Following my retirement from teaching high school math, Ray gave me the opportunity to use my skills training agents and families to put the Private Family Financing concept to work in their practice and family. This has proved to be a huge blessing to me and those I have helped.

Paul Bohlen

Private Family Financing was introduced to me by Ray in 2003 and it has become the most prominent and best financial instrument that I have known including stocks, bonds, mutual funds, and annuities. It has been something that I've been able to use to finance office equipment, vacations, and investments. It is also an avenue that allows me to get at the Federal Reserve, which I despise, and to minimally use avenues that will allow for fractional banking, which to me is a tool that allows the banks to instill a silent tax and decrease the value of our currency. Read this book and learn the process that will allow you to change your financial life forever. There is nothing better out there and I have tried them all. It is safe as any monetary instrument can be because it avoids capital gains tax, it grows tax free, and can be used without limitations. As a physician, it is my prescription to financial security only limited by your imagination.

Dr. Albert Simpkins, Jr.

Ray Poteet has been a true miracle in my life. After reading the remarkable "Becoming Your Own Banker" by Nelson Nash, I was in disbelief that it was possible to be in full control of the flow of my family's earned and investment income. Ray Poteet devoted incredible time from the start of our Private Family Finance company to help my family benefit from the incredible financial power of "The Infinite Banking Concept" as described by Nelson Nash. Application of the banking function requires guidance and support. Conventional finance wisdom before my relationship with Ray was chasing rates and terms for my life and business needs. Ray and his team at Living Wealth have transformed my life into a steady accumulation of wealth by helping my family to organize and utilize our finance process so that most of the funds that we spend for family and business flow back into our family rather than flow out of our family. Ray is always available to coach, teach and support my family as our financial circumstances change. Ray Poteet and his dedication to his clients and friends is a blessing to all who will listen and learn. This book is your blessing!! Enjoy the information knowing that it has been written by a man dedicated to your financial well-being. Enjoy the information knowing that Ray, his family and business team are experts who can guide you to live the PFF process with efficiency and confidence.

Dr. Dijkman

It was through R. Nelson Nash that I was blessed to meet Ray. I have attended a number of Private Family Financing training sessions that have marked incredible periods of my growth. Ray has been a mentor to me for a number of years. He's opened my eyes to several methods of how to take control of the banking function in our lives. Through Agent training, Ray has encouraged me to achieve business results that I didn't realize were attainable. We began capitalizing our own Family Banking System several *years ago. And with Ray's mentoring, the financial future of my family has been transformed. With 18 policies to date, our family has recaptured a 40-year $436,000 mortgage on our home in less than 7 years. In addition, we recently took a step toward building our dream home by closing on a four-acre plot of land ... a $255,000 purchase funded entirely using our own banking system. It would not be possible to express in words how grateful I am for Ray's mentoring and friendship. He gives so generously of his time and knowledge. Although we can be proud of all that we've accomplished financially by implementing Private Family Financing, we have also learned to value who we have in our lives more than what we have in our lives.*

Ray, thank you for being a terrific friend and mentor. My Family and I are very grateful for the positive impact you've had on our lives.

**In gratitude, Jayson, Rebecca, Jaxson,
Anna-Grace, Katelynn & Charlotte Lowe**

Ray Poteet has been an inspiration and shining light as to how money and our financial system really work. He has helped me to see the disconnects in the financial system and more importantly he has shown me how to communicate to my clients in a way that they can easily ascertain the truth and work towards a viable and lasting solution to their financial problems. Ray, you are truly a Blessing

.

Tim Yurek, CLU

The Tree Of Wealth

How To Build A Legacy

Raymond C. Poteet
Heather F. Graves
Holly N. Reed

Legal Disclaimer

Dedicated...

To my loving wife
&
To my wonderful daughters

ACKNOWLEDGMENTS

Thanks to Norm Baker, R. Nelson Nash, Rabbi Daniel Lapin, Rebecca Rice, Dr. Tomas P. McFie, Dr. Albert Simpkins Jr., Joe Pantozzi and Patrick Donohoe

CONTENTS

INTRODUCTION:
HOW TO USE
THIS BOOK

For a very long time, I was not quite sure what money was or what role it was meant to take on in my life. At the time, I treated money like many others do—with an unwilling respect, a healthy dose of fear, and the knowledge that there never seemed to be enough to go around.

Like a mirage, most people can see the "wealth horizon," although getting there is something entirely different. As a Christian, money was always a gray area for me. I knew I wanted enough to be financially free at some point, but the cost of living was high, and I felt like I was forced to spend everything I earned.

After working hard, my reward was to be able to afford the lifestyle I had built for my family. Of course, when you are not sure about money, it always seems to get away from you. That is how I felt back in those early days, when I still had many lessons to learn.

The good news is that I did learn them, and along my journey, I picked up some incredible insight into how money works and how I could make sure that living from paycheck to paycheck would not become my eternal fate. God wants us to lead a life of abundance, and that is really what this book is about.

I feel that when you are blessed with knowledge, it is your responsibility to pass it on so that others stand the chance to experience that "Aha!" moment like I did. This book is the product of my career, my battles with money, and the eventual victory I gained over the financial system. I am now 100% financially free.

I learned how to use car financing to turn a little into a lot, and it has made me a wealthy individual. I cannot promise you another 'sure path to riches' book, but I can tell you my story and show you how you can begin yours; and equip you with the same knowledge that brought me back to exactly where I was when I started. I started selling only life and health insurance. Then I went into the full gamut of investments, i.e., stocks, bonds, REITs, mutual funds, universal and variable life, and retirement programs. I found the truth and power of dividend paying whole life insurance in 2001 and returned to where I should have stayed all along.

Hint: Once you know how, all you need is persistence.

CHAPTER 1
THE MONEY, HONEY

"Too many people spend money they earned...to buy things they don't want... to impress people that they don't like."

Will Rogers

My name is Ray Poteet, and I will be the first to admit that I do not know everything in the world about money. Like you have no doubt found, money is a learning process. For a very long time I genuinely believed I was "doing all right" with my finances, but that was a lie.

Growing up in the working-class areas of Kansas City, my father taught me that no one owed me a living and that I would have to carve out a path for myself if I wanted it. I found this not in generating wealth for myself but for my many clients. After freeing myself from the system, I have found great pleasure in helping others do the same.

My Story

I worked hard as a young child and was an accomplished

violinist up until I lost the hearing in one of my ears. I ran track and eventually won a scholarship to the University of Kansas. There I met my wife and married her, and together we started a life. It was a typical story with typical challenges—and I was very motivated to do well in my career.

Once I had graduated from the University of Kansas with a degree in biochemistry, I became a pharmaceutical salesman. I would later go to law school, and I spent a long time selling life insurance, disability insurance, and other financial products. These performed well for my clients, but there was a class that was not being used to its fullest potential.

It was that fundamental realization that changed my life and freed me from the trappings of middle class life. I thank God for that knowledge and know that by sharing it with you, you can also orientate yourself in this financial system and rise above it. I am now my own banker, and I show my clients how to be that way too.

Today I own and run Living Wealth in Lawrence, Kansas. It is a simple company that once sold insurance then became a fully-fledged financial planning and investment firm. In 2008 it became a specialized firm dedicated to only educating individuals about Private Family Financing (PFF). I am a Chartered Financial Consultant (ChFC), a Chartered Life Underwriter (CLU), a Life and Qualifying (L&Q) member of the Million Dollar Roundtable, and a national leader in developing banks for small businesses and individuals using the Private Family Financing Concept (PFF).

The Two Types of People

I have been in finance for a long time, but I was not always financially free. It was in January 1972, ten full days before my first daughter was born, that I accepted Jesus Christ as my Lord and Savior. It was a life changing time, and only three months later my wife and I made the decision that she would not go back to work.

This was one of the most difficult decisions we have ever made. At the time, my wife earned five times more than I did. I had also changed professions recently, snagging a commission-based job in the life insurance industry. It would be the first leap of faith that I took as a Christian and the first time I trusted God with my future.

At the same time, my uncle was working for the Pentagon, and he regularly travelled between Washington, D.C., and Southeast Asia. He reached out so that we could spend some time together. This time spent with my uncle changed my life. He set me on the path to understanding money, how it works, and how wealth is truly gained.

There are two types of people in the world: people that save, and people that spend; people that use money to gain wealth and people that use money to buy things. These two groups of people are not the same; they know different things. Fundamentally, each group follows different rules about money and how it works.

Back then—when my uncle was educating me on money—I struggled to understand why the things we were told as middle-class workers were not true. Wealth—I mean real wealth—could not be gained by working hard and saving your money. I had it all wrong. I believed that I knew about financial riches, but I had no real idea yet.

Money is physical and spiritual in nature, and it needs to be treated that way. Whether you are a saver or a spender, know this; you will never get rich working in a normal job and saving as much as you can. The system no longer works that way. Perhaps it did once, but there are too many variables now.

Keeping the Money You Earn

When I would meet my uncle, he would always pose questions to get me thinking about money in a different way. "Why are you working?" he would ask. At the beginning I found it a strange question to ask because we were buying a home, we had a new baby, and I had just started out in the life insurance business.

"I work for the house, the food, the car, to build my business, and for my family," I responded, as any bright-eyed idealist would. My uncle was not impressed with my answer, however, and it vexed me. "But you could have everything you currently have and not have to work at all," he responded.

I was confused; after all, I had followed the traditional structure required for a happy, successful life. My uncle reframed his question: "Who gets all of your money?" I thought about it for a while and said, "My house, the car, our food, utilities, insurance, credit cards (I had major debt), and the church."

My uncle was once again pensive and mildly distressed. "If you do all the work and spend all the time...if it is your sweat, energy, and effort...should you not be keeping some of the money that you earn?" I did not understand what he was saying to me. I was doing what everyone else had been doing, and quite well.

I worked incredibly hard, I paid my bills, and I tried to be a good person. I could see in his eyes that I just was not getting it, but I did not know back then what I was doing wrong. Money is like that—it pretends to be something that you have, even if there is none around. That is why I love the mirage analogy—because it promises relief and provides none.

At the same time, I want you to ask yourself this question:

"Why do I not get to keep the money that I earn?" Think about it hard, and pray over it if you have to. Why is it that we have to work constantly just to spend what little we can get?

Why It Is Wise to Save

I left that meeting with my uncle feeling a little uneasy. About a month later I came across 2 Timothy 2:6: "The hardworking farmer must be first to partake of the crops." Instantly my mind shot back to that strange conversation about money with my uncle.

If you do all of the work, surely you should get to keep some of the money. The memory of the words rang through me. I suddenly understood that I had been working to give the money I earned away to everyone else. Everyone else but me.

I did not keep any of the money that I earned on a daily basis—and this was suddenly incredibly clear, like the scripture had illuminated the idea in my mind. Remember the two types of people in the world, spenders and savers?

It is not as simple as that! There are those that save and then spend and those that spend and then save. The interesting thing is that one of these groups always works for the other. People that tend to only save once they have spent nearly always work for the individuals that save first and then spend.

It is a subtle difference but a vast one in financial terms. I was the kind of person that spent all of my earned money first, then if there was any leftover, I would save it—at least until I found something else to buy with it. I was in the "worker" group, a learned behavior no doubt.

A few days later I came across another scripture, "You shall not muzzle an ox while it treads out the grain and the laborer is worthy of his wages," from 1 Timothy 5:18. This scripture would be more revealing than I thought. My perspectives were already beginning to change, and I was asking the right questions about money.

Is it wise to save? How do I save? Why do people save first and spend later? What is the difference? All I knew was that my uncle wanted me to know that saving first was wise. On the discovery of this new verse, things became clearer.

The Only Bill That Matters

If you needed to paint the outside of your home, you would hire a painter to do so. This painter would have to be paid because work is exchanged for money; that is our system. If you had to muzzle this particular ox, the ox would not be able to benefit from his labor. Because he could not eat, he could not endure any more work.

If the painter was not paid, he would not be able to feed himself, buy new brushes, or travel to the next location to continue working. The lesson that I needed to learn was that labor in today's world is paid for with money. That we can all agree on. But most people muzzle their money and do not get any real benefit from their labor.

Everyone else gets to enjoy the money earned by the painter through his extensive effort and time—everyone, that is, except the painter himself. I realized that I had been starving my spirit and that I had effectively placed a muzzle over my earnings without even realizing it.

I was not even paying myself as a laborer. Somehow, I had become a financial slave to a system I barely understood, and I had not seen it happen. Luckily, my uncle and the scripture I came across brought it together and opened my mind, and I received the truth. The truth was that I was working every day for nothing. It is not a fun truth to recognize.

Once my uncle had gone back to Washington, I began periodically asking myself, "Why are you not saving any money?" The answer to that was simple—I did not make enough money to save. I had way more bills than money because there were too many things that we needed as a family. This, however, was not entirely accurate.

As I asked myself the question more and more, I realized that I did not save any money because I did not have to. I was required to make my mortgage and car payments, and the bank did not care about anything else.

The Richest Man Anywhere

They could not have cared less if I had a good month or a bad one financially as long as my payments and fees were covered. They did not worry about a medical emergency or if my home air conditioner needed a repair job. The bank simply wanted their money, and I had agreed to a payment schedule that I kept.

My parents had always taught me to pay my bills. A good person pays their bills! I realized that I had a bill for everyone else except me, and I would not pay myself like I paid my creditors. Despite putting in all the work, all the energy, and all the effort, I was still not getting paid for my services. I failed to pay myself.

It was the one bill I needed more than any other. I bought a book, *Psycho Cybernetics* by Maxwell Maltz, that outlines how the mind works and how—through visualization—you can change your actions. That is what I needed; my actions had to change. Solomon wrote the book of Proverbs, and in 23:7 he said, "For as he thinks in his heart, so is he."

So it began in my heart, and this influenced the way I thought about things. My previous actions told me that my heart

9

believed that I was not worth anything since I did not pay myself any money. I read another book, *The Richest Man in Babylon*. From there I knew that I needed to take action and pay myself first—at least 10% of what I earned.

This was taught to all the people in Babylon, and they became the richest country in the world. Paying yourself first is life changing, and it is one thing that we practice and coach others on at Living Wealth. Based on my own realization and journey, I knew that it was God's plan for me to find financial freedom and to help you achieve it too.

You do not have to be the richest man in the world, but you do have to pay yourself first. This important rule has gone unacknowledged for too long, and it is the reason why you fail to dig yourself out of the financial abyss.

CHAPTER 2

YES, YOU CAN HAVE IT TOO (MONEY)

"Financial peace isn't the acquisition of stuff. It's learning to live on less than you make, so you can give money back and have money to invest. You can't win until you do this."

Dave Ramsey

L et's keep things honest—bankers have always owned the financial system. They were once average people like you and I that figured out a way to make a fortune off storing and protecting people's money. It is an extremely old profession.

But somewhere along the line these bankers transitioned to a system that is based on fractional banking, and that means creating money out of air or based on nothing. We no longer have currency by the gold standard, and so we are at the mercy of the bankers in power.

Money Is Not Difficult

Despite this, we are living in an unprecedented age of new technology and new wealth. Whereas many people were forced to live in poverty in the past, there is no reason why an educated person today should not end up having more than enough wealth for life if only they recognize the system for what it is and use it in their favor.

Our current monetary system[1] is a deeply complex thing. All of the money that exists is created by private banks by means of debt. The debt system came into being specifically because people no longer have to save to survive. Instead, they work to buy status symbols and put a few thousand dollars away here and there.

People never save first, and they always accrue debt in the best interests of the banks and financial companies. This is because our financial system moved from being based on the gold standard to being backed by debt.

The banks want you to owe money and a lot of it because that is their business. They are in the business of ensuring that you do not get out of the debt cycle. It is far more beneficial for them to have you spending constantly—taking out more loans and spending again —than realizing that you can keep your money debt-free and rise above the rat race.

How Money Works

Have you ever stopped to find out how money actually works? You might use money daily, but not understanding how the system works can be harmful. In the past, the entire financial system was stable because it was based on something called the

---

1 John C. Bogle, America's Financial System—Powerful but Flawed,
http://johncbogle.com/wordpress/wp-content/uploads/2006/02/Phi-Beta-Kappa-11-2-10.pdf

"Gold Standard."

Precious metals and the amount available would keep banking costs from rising to disproportionate levels. Back then, you could go into a bank and exchange all of your money for the equivalent in gold or silver.

Private banks[2] no longer lend money they have on deposit or borrow money at low interest rates to loan at higher interest rates. They create money out of thin air whenever the government or anyone takes out a loan. The transition from the gold standard to the debt system has caused economic turmoil, weakening currency and debt traps for everyone.

Banks monetize a person's promise to repay that debt by creating more money, which they store. Over time, the more money they release, the higher inflation climbs, and the more expensive trade items become. Money is a medium for exchange of goods and services, but it is also a way for the bankers to make sure they make a fortune on a debt-consumed society.

Many experts call it the "debt money system"[3] and say that it is the worst thing to ever happen to the American financial system. The bankers get billions, and the population is crippled by debt. That is why you cannot "work and save" for wealth anymore.

No amount of saving is ever going to make you rich. The entire financial system is built to encourage larger and larger debts, and once you have that, you will be working to pay it off for the rest of your life. My mortgage, my car, my credit card debt—my own debts were stacking up and preventing me from paying myself.

---

[2] Understanding Money 101, http://www.understandingmoney101.com
[3] Melvin Sickler, America's Greatest Problem – It's Debt Money System, http://www.rense.com/general75/amde.htm

Parkinson's law was in effect in my life, which is basically that expenses rise with income. I needed to live on less than I made, or I would continue to be a slave to the financial system.

The Banking System

The exact reason I could not save enough—or did not need to—was because whenever I needed extra, there was always a bank to loan me more to "cover" what I could not afford. Of course, this is no form of saving. It is a form of enslavement!

Inflation is not as "coincidental" as many Americans may believe. The truth is that all financial institutions want our current dollars (good/strong dollars) and want to pay us back with future dollars (weak dollars).

Since the shift from the gold standard[4] on August 15, 1971, by President Nixon, the American dollar has lost 75% of its purchasing power. Now there is an elite group of people that control a monopoly on printing money from nothing. Inflation has nothing to do with the greed of merchants. It has to do with a corrupt banking system left to its own devices.

The paper money that we now all use might be legal, but the exchange of good dollars for weak dollars can destroy a family's wealth. I am rich by 1970's standard but not by current day standards. Inflation has weakened my purchasing power. Inflation and keeping control of your money is a way to shift the wealth to those individuals and institutions that understand what I am trying to educate the readers of this book about.

It makes me think of the time Jesus drove the money lenders out of the temple in Matthew 21:12: "Jesus entered the temple and began to drive out all the people buying and selling animals

---

[4] Summary on How Money and the Monetary System Work,
http://www.matrixwissen.de/index.php?option=com_content&view=article&id=898:introductary-summary-on-how-money-and-the-monetary-system-work-en&catid=236&lang=en&Itemid=82

to sacrifice. He knocked over the tables of the money changers and the chairs of those selling doves."

An argument can be made that Jesus saw the unjust concept of wrongful exchange for values, a form of inflation in action, and became angered by it. It is not only a form of slavery but one that has been brought into existence by the very people that changed the system.

People all over America now believe they are free, living under a fair and just financial system like it was before 1912, only to discover more and more that their freedom is really financial slavery. They do all the work, and someone else gets all the money. People are not saving; they are in huge debt, and they need help.

Setting Up the Solution

The conventional banking system is clearly not on the side of the average American. Following the "system" is now only going to give you access to more debt, a weaker dollar, and higher taxes, which will enslave you and your family. Eventually, you will have nothing at all but the opportunity to work to pay off money you have borrowed from the conventional system.

Despite this clear and present danger to the financial wellbeing of your family, we have no choice but to work around it. That means setting up a solution for yourself that will prevent your finances from slipping into the red so badly that you cannot recover.

The solution, of course, is to be your own banker. Look after your money like the bankers look after theirs—and find methods of hanging on to the money that you earn, spend, and otherwise invest in a flawed system.

When my uncle taught me to save 10% of my income, it did

change my life. I finally started to value my work and pay myself for it. Because of that, I was able to invest and come up with flexible financial strategies that ensured my money would always return to me somehow. And that is the strategy that I and the Living Wealth team can teach you.

There are three main types of wealth in this world: the wealth that comes from your family—this is your heritage and character; the wealth that comes from God—these are spiritual gifts and wisdom that makes you unique and allows you to be who you are by using these gifts in business and with family; and material wealth—this is the assets on your balance sheet.

As a general rule, you should try to nurture all of these types of wealth in your lifetime to get the kind of rewards that God wants for you. But that requires a strategic setup and some balancing on your part. You should get to the point where you are saving at least 10% of your income each month before a single bill has been paid.

Exposing the Strategy

Working with money on a strategic level is always a solid plan. There are more wealthy financial investors than any other field in America right now. People that understand the system and know how to use it to their advantage do benefit the most.

I belong to the top 3% of my industry and have transitioned to great wealth because of these practices. I, along with the Living Wealth team, spend our days teaching our clients about these techniques so that they can conquer debt and secure their own financial futures regardless of their level of income.

Before launching into the strategy—which involves financing cars, vacations, weddings, schooling, and equipment for the office and home—we will review the three rules that make it work beforehand. Before that, a brief outline of the strategy is necessary to orient yourself in the coming process.

Private Family Financing (PFF) is a method I utilized when using life insurance to finance the assets that I bought. Even though I knew about estate planning, charitable giving, and taxes, I had never come across anything that mentioned that life insurance could be used to finance and recapture the things I normally purchased.

Life Insurance can be—and with enormous success. We are honored to say that we have helped families buy their first home and kids get into expensive colleges. We have seen our clients' lifelong dreams fulfilled because of this simple strategy that works so well.

My journey began with my first product that I purchased. I had lost money when I trusted another person with it, so I decided to invest for myself. This is what put me on the path to developing my own process that would guarantee a positive financial outcome and free me from debt and the rat-race that so many are in.

This product had to penalize me if I quit too early and reward me if I used it for a long time. I needed it to be flexible, manageable, and easy to control. I also wanted it to be safe, with decent growth and an amount that would be available instantly.

This is what ultimately led me to developing the Private Family Financing System. And it was beyond what I could have imagined back when I was slaving away and not paying myself at all. Developing the system changed my entire financial future.

Approaching Money Realistically

Money is a terribly realistic medium—you cannot escape the implications of borrowing it, owing it, or needing to lend some. The moment I began approaching it from a realistic standpoint I could develop a system that worked alongside the current system of today.

The product I eventually decided to use in the process was called "Dividend Paying Whole Life Insurance." In 1972 I had only started out in the industry—but I knew I could put my premiums (the bill I was paying to myself) on a bank draft, which allowed me to pay myself first.

I wanted to make sure that I got paid as the laborer; and if it was taken directly from my checking account, I could make sure that I paid myself first each month. If I quit early, I knew I would be penalized, but if I stuck it out and stayed, in the long run, I could benefit with each consecutive year as it guarantees to improve each year.

That process started over 40 years ago for me. The growth on my premium deposit was guaranteed each year, and I received a yearly dividend from my insurance company for each of those 40 years. I used these policies to buy cars, college educations, homes, and even pay my income taxes.

The money was available when I needed it without going through an individual that would decide if I was worthy of a loan. At the time I had no idea that life insurance had been in existence for 200 years and had been owned by many past United States presidents.

Even personalities like Walt Disney and JC Penney used these policies to start their own businesses. I am a great believer in Permanent Dividend Paying Life Insurance, and many grand things have come from these humble financial vehicles that support the statement "pay yourself first."

You will find that people are completely unrealistic about money. They make excuses about "deserving" items, which leads them to more debt and, ironically, is fueled by advertising and not genuine need. It is time that you began thinking about wealth and money in realistic terms. You may never be a billionaire, but you can still be financially free while creating a legacy for your children and grandchildren.

CHAPTER 3
THE 3 RULES OMITTED IN "GETTING RICH"

"If money is your hope for independence you will never have it. The only real security that a man will have in this world is a reserve of knowledge, experience, and ability."

Henry Ford

There are good reasons why banks have money and everyone else has debt. When you really delve into what makes a bank so profitable, you can draw lessons that will help you repair and sustain a personal banking system of your own.

To begin this process, you need to know about the three rules that are always omitted when people speak about "getting rich." Take these rules to heart, and implement their lessons in your own life to make sure that you correct your current financial problems.

The Missing Knowledge

How many books have you seen claiming to have the "secret" to wealth? I come across a lot of clients that want a lot of money but do not even understand the simplest financial terms. You cannot have great wealth unless you are an expert on money— or at least know enough to have a strategy that plays out according to plan.

I am not speaking of wealth in transient terms. These strategies will not make you a billionaire. They may not even make you a millionaire! Wealth and how much money you need to be happy is completely subjective.

You do have to concede that there are gaps in your knowledge, an uneasy feeling, like the rich and powerful know things they are not telling you. This is true. Wealthy people understand how money works and how to capitalize on this current flawed system.

While this book will only educate you on what you need to know to perform these strategies and earn long-term financial stability, your education should not stop there. I want to encourage you to embrace the idea that God wants you to "understand money and how it works."

We were not put here on earth to be slaves to this financial system or to live with almost nothing for the hard work that we put forth. If you work hard, you should receive the rewards from that work. And that means plugging some serious knowledge gaps.

Pay Yourself First (Not Later!)

Even as you read this, I know inside you are thinking about how impossible it is to save anything first, before a single bill is paid. Like me, I bet you were taught that not paying your bills first is a cardinal sin. Of course, it is right to pay what you owe—that is biblical. This is not the most important rule. Check out 2 Timothy 2:6.

You are the investment that you make each time you pay yourself.[5] When you do not pay yourself each and every month, you become overly stressed, overworked out of fear of not having enough money and social relationships degenerate. Financial stress places enormous strain on a family and your health. This never translates well.

Look at two different people as examples. Jack Wilkinson and Debbie Green both work for the same company in office administration. It is not a glamorous job, but it pays the bills (ironically). Each of them spends an average of 10 hours behind a computer every day, working hard for their pay.

When Jack gets his paycheck, he immediately spends what he has earned to pay his rent, utilities, and other bills. There is a little left over to save, but it will not last the month. Jack takes out another small loan because he has not taken a vacation in over a year and needs a break. Jack's situation continues to worsen, as upon his return he has even less money than before and no savings.

Debbie, on the other hand, always pays herself first by saving. The moment her paycheck clears, that little portion she has set aside comes off. The money itself is a comfort as she knows that in a few months she could invest in something and make more money. Debbie pays her bills afterwards and chooses not to go out.

In both scenarios, Jack and Debbie earn the same money. Debbie has transitioned to a save first then spend mindset, while Jack still feels like a rat on a hamster wheel. He has no

[5] Marisa Torrieri, Are You Paying Yourself First? The Money Habit That Can Boost Wealth, http://www.forbes.com/sites/learnvest/2014/07/24/are-you-paying-yourself-first-the-money-habit-that-can-boost-wealth/

money, lives to spend then save, and his debt and his world get smaller and smaller. In both cases, the situation will progress: Jack will sink into debt, and Debbie will rise out of it.

The Borrowers

Remember that children's movie *The Borrowers* with the tiny people that lived inside the skirting boards? They would steal bits and bobs for use but justified it by pointing out that the stuff never actually left the owner's house. Similarly, the banks lend you money from depositors, and you pay them back with interest that is greater than the bank pays the depositors.

Think about how any financial system works:

- When you borrow from a bank, you pay them interest.
- When you borrow from a credit card company, you pay them interest.
- When you borrow for a car, you pay the car company interest.

So when you pay cash for things, why are you not paying yourself interest? (Rule #2)

If you embrace the idea that you need to treat yourself like a bank, then you must see that not paying yourself interest is the same as stating that your money is not as valuable as their money might be.

Interest can be defined as the "rate" that is charged for the use of money. Every time money is used, you should be paying yourself interest to use your own money. This is a habit that can and will help you save and escalate your financial prospects over time for your release from the present financial system.

But it all begins with paying yourself first. As I have mentioned, borrowing money needs to be the same everywhere.

Do not treat yourself as any less because it is you. You are letting yourself off the hook and admitting that you are "not as important" as other money providers, which is simply not the case.

If anything, the money you have saved is *more* important than any monies secured elsewhere. That is why you need to become like a tiny borrower—when you take from yourself, make sure that you also pay yourself for it. Make sure that your money stays in your house and does not trickle out to unimportant places.

The Best Thing: EVA

This entire process is known as Economic Value Added, or EVA,[6] and it is one of our favorite things to teach our clients about. Defined, you could call it the estimation of a firm's economic profit, being the value that was created in excess of the required return.

EVA was developed based on three governing principles: that cash is king, that equity capital is expensive, and that some dollars are actually investments in disguise. When you examine the components of economic profit and determine the required calculation, it acts as a performance measure.

So EVA is the profit earned by the firm less the cost of financing the firm's capital. In the PFF system, EVA is used as a pillar and helps R.E.A.L. work for you and your family over time. I will go into more detail about this strategic system in later chapters. For now you only have to understand that EVA is not the simplest concept to understand.

In our context, EVA can be explained like this. If you borrow money from a bank, you pay the bank interest for the use of that money. The same goes for a credit card company, an auto finance company, and any other financial provider. But if you use your own money, you do not pay yourself interest. You *should*, however, be paying yourself interest; that is EVA in its simplest terms.

In Proverbs 23:7 it says, "For as he thinks in his heart so is he." We have been programmed to believe that our money is not as valuable as the bank's money and any other "creditor" that is knocking at the door. The thing is, it is still the same money. It is impossible to change your actions if your heart does not change first.

Repeat this out loud: It is all the same money. It is all important. I deserve interest too.

Even paying a small amount of interest over time can have a huge impact on your financial wellbeing. I have heard people say, "I pay cash for everything; I pay interest to no one." I respond to them by asking a question: "How old were you when you got your first car?" They answer, then I ask if they still have that car. They usually say no.

"From all the cars you have bought in your lifetime, how much of that money do you still have?" The answer is always none. I close by stating if they do not have more money than the individual who financed their car, what good did it do? Recapturing the money spent is all part of the process.

Answering the Tough Questions

In any financial strategy, you need to be able to ask the tough questions. How much does this really benefit me over time? Have I been doing X wrong for years? These questions were the same ones I had to face when I transitioned from a spender to a saver. I had to make sure those savings were in the proper system.

---

[6]Understanding Economic Value Added, http://investopeida.com/eva/

It helps a lot if you have already resigned yourself to the notion that everything is in God's control and you were meant to come across this book for a reason. Perhaps your financial ability has been lacking over the last few years. It is never too late to start over.

- How much money should you save each month? When you spend your own money, how much interest should you charge yourself?
- Treat your money like a bank does: RECAPTURE ALL YOUR INTEREST AND PRINCIPAL SO THAT YOU CAN RECYCLE IT.

It is no longer fair that banks get to have unlimited wealth while the working class has to struggle through years of debt because of the current system. Nothing is worse than starting a family and realizing how much money you will need in the coming years.

It is best you start with this strategy now so that you have enough time to wade through these uncomfortable questions early. Otherwise you will simply fall into the "debt-laden" category of the population that is essentially owned by companies and banks.

Then when the time comes to buy something you need or to retire later in life, you will not be able to without more debt, or you will not be able to at all. We are all trusting the banks to keep the financial system functioning, but that does not change the fact that they are now feeding off your money. Take control and do not fear what banks, finance companies, the government or others do, because you are in control of your own system.

Stop being a spender, and think about what that means. Switch to saving, gaining interest[7] on your own money, and recapturing the costs from the assets you buy by becoming your own specialized bank. Private Family Financing is all about this transition into long-term wealth building, and it works.

So one last question: *Are you serious about gaining financial freedom in this lifetime?*

---

[7] Herb Kitchoff, How Does Compound Interest Help You Save for Retirement?, http://finance.zacks.com/compound-interest-save-retirement-2698.html

CHAPTER 4
MY BFF IS A PFF

"Police and firefighters are great, but they don't create wealth. They protect it. That's crucial. Teaching is a wonderful profession. Teachers help educate people to become good citizens so that citizens can then go create wealth. But they don't create the wealth themselves."

Rush Limbaugh

The Best Family Friend (BFF) that you will ever develop will be a Private Family Financing (PFF) system. I know this because it took me a long time to organize and test and even longer to fully understand the freedom and repercussions that building such a process would have in my life and in the lives of the people that I loved.

Rick Warren, a prominent pastor, once said, "Life is like a marathon; it is very crowded at the start, but it thins out rather quickly." This always struck me as true, especially when it became crunch time with financial planning. Financial bondage is not like a 200 or 300-meter dash; it is like a marathon, and this marathon is called life. You *have* to assume the finish line is coming, so run the race so you will win.

Beginning the PFF Process

I, along with the Living Wealth team, have coached over 2,000 families throughout the last 13 years, and we would not have been able to do that if I had never started my own PFF process. Private Family Financing is a strategy that you need to invest in, for yourself and the good of your family. First, you have to begin the process, and that means experiencing a kind of financial cleanse.

Remember the finance muzzle? The decisions that you are making right now only work inside the debt-ridden system. The more decisions that you make that follow these unsettling rules, the closer you will get to total financial slavery. Eventually, when you turn 60, you will realize that you cannot afford to retire because you still have so much debt.

A life lived with no financial reward—either during or after your working days—is a life lived according to the debt system. That is why when I meet with a client for the first time, I always ask them one simple question:

"Do you have something in front of you? A book or piece of paper?"

"No," they nearly always reply.

Insurance for Life

Once we have found a piece of paper for them, I move to their next challenge.

"Assume that the piece of paper is a contract. If you sign this contract, you will be my slave forever. Would you sign it?"

The answer is always "Never!"

"What if I said that you would not just be my slave, but a slave to many people?"

They respond, "Still never! I would never sign away my freedom!"

"What if I told you that you are already a slave to many masters?" I say.

Nearly every time they exclaim in outrage, but I continue. "Your mortgage people, your car finance people, the food people, the gas people, the medicine people...all of these people are your masters, and they get your money. This is a hidden form of enslavement —assuming that you do not get to keep any real money after you work?"

"No, I do not have much money," they all say. There is no difference between having one master or many if that master strips you of your ability to benefit from your hard work.

"But I do benefit!" they insist. "I have a house, a car, food, and a lifestyle!" — then comes the ugly bit, the realization that sets them back — the bank owns their house. The finance company owns their car. They buy food on credit. They live on borrowed money that is thrown into a bottomless black pit, never benefitting them in any measurable way.

My job, along with the Living Wealth team, is to teach people like you that despite the quiet nature of your enslavement, by the very definition you are still enslaved. Working to enrich someone else for no real personal benefit *is* slavery—the most insidious kind.

It has been called the "financial awakening"[8] because so many people are realizing that it is all wrong. Yet the only people able to dig themselves out of it are the ones that learn to

---

[8] The Number One Tool of Financial Enslavement,
http://theeconomiccollapseblog.com/archives/tag/financial-enslavement

work with the system instead of for it.

The good news is that while the system is broken, we are also living in a special time of enlightenment and knowledge sharing. God is making sure that those that seek out answers will find them. That means you only need to realize it to force change.

The Stark Realization

Think about long-term finance for a moment. Does it last for 10 years, 30, 500? Should wealth not be a family concern and a generational development point? If you can learn how to make your PFF into your family's BFF, then you need not suffer as economic slaves or be concerned with the stock market and how it is doing.

This is the greatest gift that you can pass onto your children and one that will benefit them throughout their lives. Ask yourself, "How long have you been working for a living?"

It is a tough question because when you look back at all the time you have spent, you begin to realize that this time has not been converted into financial freedom but financial slavery. Our clients usually say anything from "two months" to "60 years."

Then we ask them another question, and we are going to ask you the same question now:

"Are you worth $2.50 an hour if you are an hourly or salary employee?"

"Are you worth $250.00 per day as an owner of a garage?"

"Are you worth the cost of a patient visit a day if you are a physician, dentist, or chiropractor?"

Then we take your average work hour and place it along a 10-year timeline. Quickly and easily, we multiply the number of years you have worked by $5,000.00. Here's how:

$2.50/\text{hr} \times 8\text{hr}/\text{day} = \$20/\text{day} \times 5 \text{ days} = \$100/\text{wk} \times 50/\text{wks} = \$5,000.00/\text{year}$

Can you write me a check for $50,000 right now?

If you said "no," hey, you are not alone. Some 98% of our clients cannot write out a $50,000 check because they just do not have it—even after working for decades. They realize or are saying, "I did all the work, and everyone else got all the money. I really have been a slave."

For most of our clients, this is a stark realization that after so much time invested in working, they have no financial security or comfort—absolutely no wealth at all. This is the perfect starting point because it helps you realize that what you have been doing is wrong.

Pride and believing that what you are doing is the right thing are nothing if there is no evidence to back it up. Even the proudest man has to admit that after so much time has passed, if they have no money (keeping score), they clearly are not following the right financial system.

Making someone else rich[9] was not doing the same for them.

Everyone Needs a Wise Uncle

My life would be very different now if my uncle had not stepped in and mentored me. He asked me the questions I could not have asked myself at the time, because my limited perspective prevented me from even realizing that there was a problem.

You see, middle class people are told to be happy with what they have.[10] They believe that money is the root of all evil, which is not scriptural. People with wealth, however, know that

---

[9] Jeff Haden, The Only Way to Get Really, Really Rich, http://www.inc.com/jeff-haden/the-only-way-to-get-really-really-rich.html

[10] Mandi Woodruff, 21 Ways Rich People Think Differently, http://www.businessinsider.com/how-rich-people-think-differently-from-the-poor-2012-8?op=1

poverty is evil, and they do all they can to convert money they have into assets that will create a legacy for their family. Middle-class Kevin will buy himself a car. Wealthy David would rather buy a car and repay to his own PFF the principal and interest, thus recapturing all the money so it can be recycled on the item that his family wants or needs.

You have been working for everyone else's benefit. They pay you money so that you can exchange your time for their vision of gaining more wealth. That is the trade off—which is why you follow their rules and policies. When both a husband and wife are working, which is what happens at least half of the time, then they should be saving at least $5.00 an hour ($2.50/hr for each) into their PFF system.

If this is not happening—and none of this money is being saved into a PFF program—then there is no doubt in my mind that you have unwittingly bought into the debt system that will keep you in some form of financial slavery. Whether you like it or not, economic slavery is your reality if you do not change.

It is the reason why when the 20th comes each month, you fall short of money. It is why there is always another outstanding bill that needs to be paid. I personally believe that everyone in the world needs a wise uncle like I was fortunate enough to have.

Someone needs to stop the repeated earn-and-spend loop to say, "Hey! Are you happy with this? Do you know what is happening to your money?" It is not enough to save after the bills are paid, as we understand now, that this will never make us rich. Instead, those of you who genuinely want to pursue financial freedom need an aggressive financial plan.

Scripture to Live By

Money is not evil, but it is a myth that has been perpetuated and inspired by the mass media for many years. I personally believe that the journey to wealth is long and treacherous, and it is dotted with many trials. You have to become the kind of person that understands money and the intense responsibilities and stressors that come along with it.

It is far easier to be bad with money than to be good with it. That said, God has walked with me on this journey, guiding each step that I have taken. I know in my heart that there has been a miscommunication about money and its relevance in our modern lives today. Far from being the root of all evil, it is actually the most direct path to freedom.

There are many, many scriptures that support this argument, and I have held them close over the years, even through my most trying times. "But seek ye first the kingdom of God and his righteousness, and all these things will be added to you." Matthew 6:33[11] speaks of keeping God at the center of all your dealings so that prosperity can happen.

The Lord wants you to lead a full and abundant life, and this is further reinforced by Romans 12:2, which says, "Do not be conformed to this world, but be transformed by the renewal of your mind, that by testing you may discern what is the will of God, what is good and acceptable and perfect."
When you keep God at the center of your financial success, great things do happen. And this is proven over and over again as you find yourself freed from the former restraints of a broken system. I live by these scriptures and more, which I know to be true. The path may not be easy, but for those willing to walk on it, there are endless rewards.

I placed faith in God many years ago and achieved more wealth as a direct result of this very simple belief system.

---

[11] Abundant Life, http://www.openbible.info/topics/abundant_life

God first, money second. I no longer believe that God wants us all to be poor and humble but rather humble to God despite any financial circumstance. It is less common to find a humble rich man than it is a humble poor man.

The Fault in Your Finances

You can no longer claim to be left in the dark without a helping hand. God places people (and books) in our path so that we can learn from others and elevate ourselves. I urge you to stop buying into the old notions of money and to stop thinking of financially stable people as "evil," "lucky," "wicked," or "crooked."

Wealth is something that is earned and maintained over time, using good decision making, knowledge, and help from people that know a little more than you do. I was influenced by my uncle, by mentors, and by the many authors who wrote books leading me down this winding path.

Now I am sitting here writing my own book in the hope that it will jar you out of this media-induced false sense of security.[12] My greatest wish is for you to stop, to take account of your actions. The people around you are not working in their own best interests.

They are the workers, the spenders, the bill-paying good people that later save a little and stash it away like money is a rare commodity. This is a mindset that can and must shift, and you have the opportunity now to do it. I believe God places these opportunities in our lives to prompt us to action. So…

- There is fault in your financial situation.
- You are working to enrich others and not yourself.
- You will never become financially stable doing what you are doing now.
- You need help.

Allow this book to jolt you out of that oblivious state that you have been living in. Do not simply close the book or click away to endure yet another decade of poverty. I do not promise you fancy cars and unlimited wealth, but I can promise you more peace.

Together, using the Private Family Financing system, we will build you a transparent, easy-to-understand financial plan that will benefit you and your kids financially for generations. Turn the mistakes that you have been making into learning experiences.

I, along with the Living Wealth team, am holding out my hand to you. I want you to take it.

---

[12] 6 Facts You Have to Face If You Want to Be Rich, http://www.huffingtonpost.com/wise-bread/6- facts-you-have-to-face-_b_4380802.html

CHAPTER 5

CALCULATE YOUR WAY TO PERFECT WEALTH

"Be careful to leave your sons well instructed
rather than rich, for the hopes of the instructed
are better than the wealth of the ignorant."

Epictetus

For every financial ambition, there is a product that can
assist you on the road to perfect wealth. Working with
finance over the years has taught me that if you get to know
the numbers well enough, you can make magic happen with
them.

The product that I use to build my clients' wealth, which is
part of my Private Family Financing system, is a Dividend
Paying Whole Life policy issued by a mutual company. This
policy is the cornerstone in the financial approach that I
invested in and guide my clients through when they are
actively seeking out

real solutions to long-term poverty.

What Is a DPWL Policy?

A DPWL policy,[13] as we call it for short, is a type of permanent cash value life insurance that provides you benefits for your "whole" life. This is in sharp contrast to term insurance, which only lasts for an allotted amount of time. The policy pays you dividends each year, and this kind of life policy has a guaranteed, pre-set annual cash value increase.

Of course, how your financial partner or team designs the product determines how well it will work with your own PFF system. That is why selecting a financial coach or company that is familiar with designing and using these policy types is essential.

At Living Wealth, for example, the coaches and staff have been trained to design the correct policy to use for your specific system. This policy needs to be designed for financing first and foremost and then for death benefit purposes—not the other way around.

Your DPWL policy needs to be created according to your financial situation. With a mindful, skilled financial coach, you can structure your policy in a way that benefits you every time you need to make a purchase. This simple step alone can ensure that you are working the system in a way that will benefit you for life.

The PUAR + DPWL Equation

Within the realm of designing Dividend Paying Whole Life policies, most of them are specifically built for death benefit

---

[13] What Is Dividend Paying Whole Life Insurance, http://www.bankonyourself.com/what-is-dividend-paying-whole-life-insurance

alone. For this reason, the traditional structure fails to account for the Paid Up Additions Rider, or PUAR, vehicle.

Bear with me, if you can—these financial products are all part of the system that will help you achieve financial freedom, but you need to understand each product part first.

A PUAR vehicle[14] is a part of the infinite banking concept that my firm abides by. These are an immediate purchase of life insurance coverage in full. The paid up insurance then adds cash value equal to the paid up price. You do not have to pay any premiums or insurance costs.

When you add a PUAR to your DPWL equation, magic can happen. That is why when you choose to work with a financial coach, it always gives you peace of mind if that coach has adopted the same method for gaining wealth as that coach proposes to you. Financial coaches at Living Wealth use these vehicles to gain wealth for their own families.

Your coach needs to be proficient in training others based on the financial victories that he has won in his own financial process. It is not simply one victory that matters but a series of victories that are daily, monthly, and annually benefitting you.

This carefully selected coach will guide you through the maze of financial arenas so that you get to understand what victory feels like instead of only hearing about it in passing. With this equation, you will be able to understand the moving parts of your system as they are governed and monitored by a trustworthy coach.

It is important that you understand each step in your Private Family Financing system. This will help you transition to becoming your own banker, where you will learn how to use money in a way that earns you more instead of putting you in

---

[14] What Are Paid Up Additions, http://www.becomingyourownbank.com/infinite-banking-what-are-paid-up-additions/

debt.

Financial Freedom by Design

It is true that financial freedom does not happen accidentally. It is a very purpose-orientated act. That is why the proper design of your DPWL and PUAR will be the first real workout that you are made to endure as part of your rigorous financial training that the coaches at Living Wealth will put you through.

Having the right design at this point is like dropping into a shoe shop to choose some shoes before the start of an intense gym session. If you choose the wrong shoes to work out in, your feet will get injured, and you will not get the maximum benefit from your workout.

It makes sense, then, to ensure that you choose durable running shoes over stilettos, boots, or spikes. In the same way, the financial coaching that you choose will determine how your DPWL and PUAR are structured.

You need the proper product balance that a well formulated DPWL and PUAR bring and one that has been designed specifically for you and your family's needs. You will always set specific objectives first that are unique to your circumstances and situation, and these will guide the decisions that are made about your PFF system.

If you make the mistake of choosing the wrong coach and get the wrong design, it will leave you fatigued and disinterested in continuing your financial training. I admit that this type of financial training is much like playing sports; if you skip practice, then the coach may not allow you to play in the game.

With financial training,[15] you will gain a lot of victories if you are consistent with your training and listen to your coach. This is ultimately financial freedom by design—but it is a two-way street. You need expert opinion and guidance, but you also need the self-responsibility required to do your own training on the subject.

The inevitable victory will be straightforward—you will be able to buy that new car, go on that extended family vacation, pay your kids' college tuition, and pay your income tax—while recovering the entire cost of each transaction. This is the greatest victory that the coaches of Living Wealth can train you to reach.

The Real Benefit of This Equation

The real benefit of this equation is that you will finally be able to afford the things that you have wanted most without losing the money you have worked so hard to earn all along. And all it takes is a partnership with the right financial coaching team.

The right product with the right design can do amazing things for your family finances. I will go into some detail about how this is done a little later on in this book. For now, recognizing the benefit of this equation is important for the next step.

There are too many families that are not taking advantage of their Dividend Paying Whole Life policies.[16] These are incredible for a few very important reasons. First, all premiums that you end up paying into your policy have real cash values that are guaranteed. Because the value is guaranteed, you will not be subject to fluctuating interest rates or market volatility.

This cash value growth is not considered taxable income under the IRS code, so your dividends can be used to increase the value of your life insurance policy so that you can pass on greater wealth to your kids.

---

[15] Scott Holsopple, The Importance of Financial Literacy,
http://www.fool.com/retirement/general/2014/08/28/the-importance-of-financial-literacy.aspx
[16] Leslie Scism, Life Policies: The Whole Truth,
http://online.wsj.com/articles/SB10001424052702303296604577450313299530278

Finally, as you place your money into the cash values to work for you, the insurance company will still pay you dividends on your policy. These are used to purchase more face value (death benefit) in the policy, and again, the current growth is tax deferred.

This policy becomes a major asset as you can withdraw or borrow money based on what you have put into it. Remember pay yourself first? This is where your money will go when you do. The benefits are extensive, and the more you understand how this system works, the more impressed with it you will become.

The end result is a specific method of rapidly improving your wealth over time. It is also true that in order to achieve this, you have to become a new person over time. What I mean by this is that you need to become the kind of person who deserves this wealth and can manage it adequately.

Skyrocketing Your Wealth

It is true that a DPWL and PUAR that are structured correctly can skyrocket your wealth in a PFF system. Just adding the PUAR to your DPWL allows your financial coach to prepare you for victory in a much, much faster manner than a conventional DPWL design ever could.

The moment you add that PUAR to your policy, you can start the financing process sooner, and you will not have to work any harder or change your current cash flow situation.

When I explain it to potential clients, I always use the space shuttle analogy. Think of your DPWL and PUAR as a space shuttle ready to blast off into space. Your DPWL is your shuttle, and your PUAR are your specially designed rockets that will blast the shuttle into space.

So you have your Saturn rocket and your two Titan rockets

that will launch your shuttle into orbit around the earth. The shuttle itself is smaller than the rockets, but it needs their assistance to get it off the ground and push it against gravity to reach outer space.

In the same way, a DPWL needs the PUAR to get it off the ground at first. When your DPWL reaches space, its mission is not over, but the PUAR rockets can fall away because their job is done. A space shuttle needs engineers to design those incredible rockets so that the shuttle can reach that mission location.

Your PFF system needs a financial team to design your DPWL and PUAR to achieve a similar effect so they can guide you through your PFF processes. Imagine finally reaching space, and you are hit by a meteor shower! Without a finance team to guide you through the rough patches, you are much more exposed to risk.

You can get this balance right in your PFF system with God's help and by partnering with a dedicated finance team that wants to help you achieve victory over your current circumstances.

Skyrocketing your wealth is a conscious choice and a consistent practice. Ask any of our financial team members who invest in their own PFF system, and they will tell you what it takes to keep your family finances in the green, moving forward regardless of the current economic situation.

The Only Route Is Ahead

I do not agree with the statement that "wealth only makes you more of what you already are." This might be true in some ways, but on the whole,[17] wealth is not something you can just decide to have that never changes you in any way.

The road ahead is long and fraught with many dangers,

especially in the financial world. You have to become a better version of yourself if you want to make the change permanent. As you are now, your beliefs, ideals, and practices abide by a different set of rules.

Becoming the kind of person that understands money and how it works as well as how to "get rich" buying cars like I did using these various vehicles requires dedication, the right policies, and a trustworthy financial team. Death cannot be avoided, so you have to plan for it as a known risk, which is much safer than planning for some indefinable future.

At the same time, you might as well plan around that eventuality. The only route lies ahead for you, and you will have to ask some uncomfortable questions to get there.

Do you trust yourself to plan for your financial future?

Most people say "no" or "yes" with a look of hope and confusion on their face. Instead of leaving it to chance, I want to challenge you to not leave it to chance. Your insurance company is not going to make wealth happen for you. Only you and your chosen financial coach can do that over time with the right decisions and with constantly monitoring your PFF GPS plan.

The bottom line is that wealth is no more evil than poverty is a virtue. You have lived through lean times and felt the suffering that it brings. Inevitably you will age, and your wants and desires will change. You need to make sure that your finances grow with you, or you may end up in a situation where you never have enough money for anything.

Keep your eyes on God, and invest the time required to making sure that your chosen financial coach sits with you and

---

[17] Dr. Tomas P. McFie, Prescription for Wealth, Page 3

44

consciously designs a PFF system that will guarantee you improved wealth and stability over time.

CHAPTER 6
WEALTH IN THE FAST LANE

"Whoever renders service to many puts himself
in line for greatness —great wealth, great return,
great satisfaction, great reputation and great joy."

Jim Rohn

When you pursue wealth, it is like living life in the fast lane because of the sheer number of decisions that need to be made that can impact your entire life. Once you have realized that you need to change fundamentally in order to become wealthy, the next question becomes—how? A good financial coach should have a lot to say about that.

At this point in your PFF system planning and set up, you have your DPWL and PUAR equation that will help kick off your financing model. From here, you need to choose which products you can use to accelerate your wealth—cars, shows, restaurants, vacations, weddings, education, homes, and life insurance. You get to choose.

Picking Your Product Expert

I am a huge NASCAR fan. I love the competitive nature of the sport, the drivers and their ambitions, and the technical sets that are invested in everything from tweaking engine performance to which lines are the best to hug around the track.

Jeff Gordon[18] is my favorite driver, and he drives for Chevrolet whenever there is another tournament or challenge. The car itself was designed for peak performance and is tuned and tweaked consistently before each race.

I also have a car, but it is not a race car and was never designed for racing. When I put my foot flat down on the accelerator, sure, I can go fast. But if I ever had to pitch up at the track one day and challenge Jeff Gordon, he would certainly win.

The reason why he would win is because his car was designed by NASCAR engineers and technicians and experts to run in NASCAR races. Even if we had to design a car for NASCAR, Jeff Gordon would still win—because he knows the process of the product better than I would know it.

In other words, Jeff is more comfortable in the fast car than I would be, despite going to the trouble of getting my car designed for NASCAR. There is no better method of being prepared than choosing a highly specific product and learning the process of how to use it.

Designing Your PFF Policy

The design of your PFF policy is extremely important as it is meant to protect your money from inflation and other risks that you should not be willing to take with your money. It is time to

---

[18] 24 Jeff Gordon, http://www.nascar.com/en_us/sprint-cup-series/drivers/jeff-gordon.html

accept that we live in a government mandated economy, and we should act accordingly.

That means finding the delicate balance between living within the system and living outside or apart from the system. Taxes will always be tricky and something that is tough to control, so stick with a coach that gets you the right structure and best possible policy.

Because you are becoming your own banker, you will learn to understand things like taxes and how they will impact the profit you make using the PFF system over time. You will see that when you control these invisible numbers, they can increase your profits, therefore increasing your cash available and your legacy.

At the same time, it is your responsibility to teach your children to protect their assets from people that want to own them using debt as an enslavement tool. It is important to separate your money from the money that the "takers" are removing from your account every month.

Your Dividend Paying Whole Life policies become this separate place where you can make sense of your money and use it to perform for you. Simply setting money aside in this vehicle will protect you from the rampant losses that can occur when your money sits in a bank account you do not control.

In this way, your PFF policy becomes like your own personal banking system. You are sheltered from the costs and taxes that eat away at your money, and you can use your policy in creative ways to expand your wealth using compound interest, savvy investing, and knowledge about reclaiming money that you spend on assets.

As always, the success of your PFF policy rests on your shoulders and on the shoulders of the financial coach that you choose to partner with. The two of you alone will be able to build wealth for you over time. Without the coach, your race car will be without an experienced driver, and without you, there will not be a manager making the big decisions.

The Age Analogy

The team at Living Wealth designs products for our clients all the time, and we do so in a way that incorporates their specific circumstances and goals with our keen knowledge and insight on the vehicles being used. The results have been rewarding for our clients.

There are so many factors to consider when designing your PFF policy. It needs to be the most efficient and productive version of itself possible, so a leading and primary factor that you must have is the team and your coach.

Your policy must be designed to finance everything that you and your family do so that you can recapture the cost of those activities. That is right, I said "recapture." This system works to ensure that when you spend, you also have a method of getting back the money that you spent, ensuring your eventual financial growth and wealth accumulation.

Many people believe that it is better to use a young person because the true insurance costs are less if you are younger. The truth, however, is that financing does not impact age, and it is not as big a factor as companies have made it out to be.

I have personally worked with patriarchs and matriarchs as old as 80, and while their age was a factor, they had kids in their fifties and sixties, so we could design a policy for them that would help them achieve their objectives anyway.

These older clients also had grandchildren in their thirties and forties. What you need to understand is that when a person enters a financial institution to make a deposit, the teller does not ask how old you are because it does not matter.

The bankers and owners want you to deposit your money in their institution no matter how old you are. Your PFF system will work in the same manner, and when you look closely, you will realize that age is just a factor, not an obstacle.

Why Health Comes Before Wealth

If I, for example, had to take a 63-year-old man, a 49-year-old man and a 21-year-old woman and place $10,000 each year into each of their savings accounts at the same institution, then at the end of five years, who do you think would have the most money?

They would all have the exact same amount.

So you see, age is just a factor. It does not govern the success that you have with this PFF system. It is beneficial despite your age! The only time age matters is when your policy is being designed. Then age will play a small role with a conventional DPWL that does not have a PUAR attached to it.

With the policies mentioned above for the three groups of people, what really matters will be the money that they have to invest. The 49-year-old man has $600.00 more cash than the 63-year-old man and $3,900.00 more than the 21-year-old female at the end of those five years. Each individual has invested $10,000 for five years and the amount of cash varies because of age, but not a great amount of cash.

These cash differences have never prevented these individuals from moving forward and partnering with us or being trained by us during their financing journey. All great athletes have coaches to hold them accountable and to spot the small errors that are made along the way—which is what talented financial coaches do when they are training you in the PFF model.

After age, health is the biggest factor in insurance.[19] While the financial institution never asks about the health of an individual, they only pay attention if that person can no longer pay their deposits every month. Otherwise, as long as the payments are being made, they could not care less.

It is entirely possible to take a policy that is rated and to design it to have close to the same amount of cash as a healthy individual that is of the same age and sex. For example, a male client at age 38 was a smoker and diabetic—and my team at Living Wealth designed him a policy that matched his choice to be a non-smoker at that age.

Connecting the Dots

There are many other factors that can limit your insurance coverage. Things like driving records, sports that you enjoy (scuba diving, motor racing, and rock climbing for example), and the like can be influencing factors in the design process.

You have to be able to connect the dots for your finance coach. We are able to design a product for you that will work with your objectives—most of the time. Many other quality financial providers will be able to do the same if you ask them too.

If there are any limitations, we will let you know. When this happens, and the company refuses, you will be notified, and we can work around it. The key thing is that when you begin your private family financial training, your coach should be there to jump each hurdle with you, coach you through each race, and sprint with you towards your chosen experiences.

Staying on course is a goal that great financial coaches always keep in mind. This allows them to connect the dots along with

---

[19] Robert J Doyle, Keith A Buck, 10 Things to Know About Whole Life Insurance, http://www.lifehealthpro.com/2014/09/15/10-things-to-know-about-whole-life-insurance

you so that the partnership is mutually beneficial. This is the reason why Living Wealth designs a PFF GPS.

Then your coach[20] will use your PFF GPS to guide you and register your progress. I like to think of it as a checkpoint system used in the race we call LIFE. The plan outlines where the destinations or dots will be, and you will know exactly how to get there and what will happen when you do; it also allows for flexibility and change because we know life is not static.

All that remains is to continue along your path, to keep an eye on any changes, and to slowly trace in the lines of the track to form the full picture. When you are done, you should be able to see the plan clearly—how it worked and why—and you will be able to enjoy the rewards from it and create a legacy you had only dreamed about previously.

Connecting the dots in the PFF system is a great way to view collaboration between you and your coach. It will be a learning process for both of you, and the closer you get to a perfect design, the better off your system will be.

Your Own PFF System

If you have made it this far, you are excited about the possibilities that Private Family Financing can have in your life. All it takes is an understanding of the process that comes after the decision has been made.

Do you believe that being your own banker is important in this day and age? Do you want to begin your private family financing system?

Then this is the beginning for you.

Starting your own Private Family Financing System is very simple once you have applied for and received our DPLW and PUAR policies. They are essential elements in the system.

---

[20] Practitioner Finder, http://www.infinitebanking.org/finder/

The coaches over at Living Wealth will help you develop your very own PFF GPS. This is the tool that really shakes things up and begins to transform the way you use money in your daily life.

You will know where you are with money right now, which is not always an easy reality to face. Then you will be shown where you are going financially by your chosen financial coach. Your coach will use this information to see how you are progressing with the financial workouts that the coach sets for you.

Remember, self-responsibility and knowledge are a big part of getting financial planning right. You cannot expect your coach to do it all for you or your insurance company to "make it happen" without you.

You are ultimately the decision maker, and if you are not well oriented in what is happening with your money, then you cannot expect to become wealthy. It is that simple—really. Being wealthy means being responsible and informed.

We work with people from all walks of life who know they want to be financially free. "I want to have at least $150,000 disposable money," they will say. There is always an amount, but rarely do we find clients that fully understand where they are currently with their finances.

There is often debt, struggle, and no money when we step in to fix the problem. Your PFF system will be designed around your goals and where you want to be financially as you get older. You will actively dig yourself out of the financial pit until you can float away on the waves of financial freedom.

CHAPTER 7
THE PROCESS OF WEALTH BUILDING

"The real source of wealth and capital in this new era is not material things...it is the human mind, the human spirit, the human imagination, and our faith in the future."

Steve Forbes

A GPS, or global positioning system, was designed to provide location and time information to people that were traveling from one location to the next. Keeping track of where you are going is the underlying principle involved in GPS technology. When you always know where you are, you can never become lost.

Because of this, any decision that you make tends to be more accurate, with less risk and a much greater chance of eventually reaching your final destination. The process of wealth building requires these features—*consistency, tracking, and monitoring*—so that you can maximize the benefit of this financial plan.

Your Finance Plan: Cruise Control

If you could design the perfect financial plan for yourself, I bet it would be one that you could "set and forget." This is the default requirement for many people because their lives are already so busy. People simply do not have the time to spend focusing on their finances every other day and making complicated adjustments.

But cruise control in finance does not exist. There are only two kinds of financial plans—the ones that you monitor and they improve and the ones that you do not monitor and they end up losing you money. The "set and forget" principle has been stripping people of their savings for many years. It is dangerous and unwise to think things do not change.

That is why we explain your new Private Family Financing plan as a vehicle that has been programmed with a specific GPS route. It shows you where you are and how to get from that point to where you want to be in the future.

It works because at all times you know exactly where you are. Have you ever been driving somewhere and suddenly hit a gridlocked area? The only way to escape it is to take a different route. The risk is there that you may become lost. A PFF GPS setup makes sure this never happens to you with your money.

What is a PFF GPS?

A PFF GPS is a tool that lays out the roadmap you will take when you start your PFF system. The worst thing you could do would be to get started and yet have no idea how to implement Private Family Financing! That would be like hopping in the car to go on vacation without having any idea where you're going and then realizing that you left your maps and GPS at home!

We design for you, your very own PFF GPS to illustrate how to implement your system in your specific situation-whether it's helping you navigate your way to becoming debt-free, displaying the most efficient route to pay for your child's education, or simply demonstrating how you can afford to pay for vacations, cars, weddings, or the many other "detours"that present themselves along the way. With your GPS, you will always know the best plan of action to seer through life's many changes.

The Car GPS Analogy

When you track your Private Family Financing System, your GPS is always on. When you take a left turn, you simply plug in the new details of your altered destination, and away you go. Turn after turn, landmark after landmark, eventually you will reach that destination.[21]

The reason that you can change where you want to go and still arrive there safely is that the GPS always knows where you are on the road while the change is happening. However, if your GPS thought that you were in a different state and gave you those directions, you would become hopelessly lost. It would not work.

I know this from personal experience. On arrival at a car rental center while away on business, I hooked up my GPS, and what do you know—it thought I was still back home, before I climbed on the airplane. It suggested a number of unrelated and strange routes before it went blank and read "acquiring satellites."

While it realized that I was not where I once was, it calibrated where I was currently. Once it had established that, it set a new course based on the new maps it has sourced. In order for the

---

[21] Kate Brodock, Financial Know-How Is Important for Both Personal and Professional Success, http://www.forbes.com/sites/katebrodock/2014/01/26/financial-know-how-is-important-for-both-personal-and-professional-success/

GPS to get me exactly where I needed to go, it had to find me first. It is not enough to simply know where you want to be.

This is a mind shift from what you may be used to. A lot of clients have lofty goals, but it does not reflect in their current financial situation—like they have chosen not to assess their finances because they are such a mess. Because of this, anything they have tried has failed because the GPS cannot get a fix on their location.

In the same way, your Private Family Financing System is an always-on GPS. At all times you know what you have and where you want to be. It sounds easy, and yet most people do not establish the first step in this process. Begin thinking of your financial plan as a GPS system that comes with built-in warnings about potential financial routes.

Extending the Equation

Your PFF GPS will work in the same way as your car GPS does. One works financially while the other works geographically, but the functions are similar. With Private Family Financing, you will find out where you are financially right now.

It is a difficult assessment, but it is also a very relevant one. From there, you can plan your route, so to speak, or map your financial course. The coaches at Living Wealth, for example, will help you determine your exact financial position.

We will work together on planning the best route forward— a route that will take you towards your goals and objectives with every year that passes. When you map out your route that way, it extends the equation and makes it feasible.

Once your initial map is outlined with various pit stops, sights to see, and milestones, you will be able to use it as a benchmark plan.

- Will your mapped-out route ever change?
- Can you change this route at any time?
- Should you change your route?

The answer to all of these questions is a resounding "Yes!"

The PFF is not a "set and forget" model, because those do not work for long-term investing. Instead, you will have a map laid out before you that is easy to adjust, change, and tweak as you come across different obstacles in your life.

Flexibility and options come with this financial plan, along with the certainty that your end goal—the final destination—is programmed in, and you will still reach it regardless of any gridlock detours.

Studies have been performed in the financial industry[22] that have proven financial monitoring improves eventual outcomes, and this formula must be applied to your plan too. Treating your system like your own bank calls for this, and it also calls for a greater level of participation, tracking, and monitoring of your progress.

The good news is that this extension is worth its weight in effort and returns. While the PFF requires it, it also ensures that your GPS will always let you know where you are financially.

Why It Takes Lifelong Planning

I am sure you have heard someone say "'the sooner you start saving, the better off you will be." This is an old adage that comes from the pre-war years when our currency was a lot stronger and inflation and taxes were not so complex and ever-changing.

---

[22] Sridhar Ramamoorti, The Benefits of Continuous Monitoring,
http://raw.rutgers.edu/docs/wcars/23wcars/presentations/Mike%20Cangemi-
The_Benefits_of_Continuous_Monitoring_edited_final_8-11[1].pdf

But it is true that wealth takes lifelong planning. The only thing we have of any real value is the time we get in this world. The PFF system helps you convert your working time into real wealth during your lifetime, and it will also benefit your children one day.

Now, you have your main product, which is your DPWL and PUAR, which you will capitalize soon. Then you need to add your PFF GPS. This capitalization phase of your PFF is a lifelong process, so it is never something that is done once and never again.

Many of my clients first believed that their policy was only an investment, but based on Proverbs 23:7[23] (For as he thinks within himself, so he is), this thinking needs to shift from product investment to a process that needs to happen.

The coaches at Living Wealth have been taught the importance of changing this single thought process in our clients. Imagine this for a second. You are back in college, and you have to choose what to study. I studied biochemistry— what did you study?

How much money did you earn from your first year of college while studying in your specific field? The answer is almost always "zero." How about year two? Year three? Year four? Chances are during your study years you did not earn a penny from your chosen field.

Now answer this question. Did it cost you any money to go to school for these four or five years? Did you have to take out any loans to get through school? The answer is commonly "yes."

What happened during this study process is that you capitalized your education so that you could work in a

---

[23] Proverbs 23:7, https://www.biblegateway.com/passage/?search=Proverbs%2023:7

profession that pays you more one day. (That was your thought anyway; I thought I wanted to be a doctor.) You took out a loan (or someone paid for it) to educate yourself for the future chance of being paid better, correct?

The goal with the Private Family Financing system is to share with you how to capitalize on and create your own financial system that works. It is a series of policies, not just one investment vehicle, and it needs to be allowed to grow into your end goal.

The Business Analogy

If you are still not sure what I mean, I have an analogy for that too. Think of a common business setup. If you go into business, you often need to buy land, design and build a building, or lease a space from someone else.

You will either need to build that building or do tenant improvements on the lease location. Once this is sorted out, you will purchase the right furnishings, computers, telephones, and equipment, and you will hire and train your staff.

Then once you have sorted out your staff benefit packages, you will have to do some advertising and marketing to inform the public that you are in business.

Have you earned any money yet or just spent money?

Did you spend and capitalize this business to make a profit?

You can only do one of those things, and most often it is just spending money. Living Wealth's coaches, and others like us, train you to capitalize your PFF system so that it becomes profitable as quickly as possible based on how you use it. Your PFF can finance everything you and your family buy and recapture every dollar so it can be recycled, just like the conventional banks currently operate.

It is designed as a process that will get better every year if you follow your coach's directions and do everything that they request from you in your training routines. After all, you will determine how well this process works regardless of any economic conditions.

You are in complete control of those end results. This is a massive change from previous concepts and strategies that tell you to transfer and lose control of your money to someone else. This is not self-responsibility, and it does not lead to improved outcomes.

It is true that financial coaches are experts in their field. But it is also true that you should aspire to be an expert too. Experts cannot do better things with your money than you can. Only you fully understand your situation, your needs, and the risks you are willing to take.

The PFF system is innovative because it places the power back where it belongs—with you. Personal responsibility[24] is something that has been side-lined and downplayed too long in the financial field. How can anyone achieve real success without being involved? It is not possible, and it only leads to missteps and disappointment.

Annual Wealth Building Marathon

The truth is that if you have not been trained in the PFF process, then there is no guarantee that your finances will get better and better each year. Your coach should make that empirically clear to you.

I know this because I once followed a process that excluded self-responsibility and was part of the "hand over" or "set and forget" model. I gave them money and lost control of it to the

---

[24] Kitchen Table Finances: New Survey Reveals Increased Personal Financial Responsibility Among Americans With Goals to Save More and Reduce Debt, http://www.newyorklife.com/about/kitchen-table-finances-new-survey-reveals-increased-personal-financial-Responsibility-among-americans-

person I thought would do better than I could. I lost a lot of money this way.

But since 2001, when I kept control and started practicing what my PFF coach taught me, I not only made a lot of money, but I recaptured all the money for the item that I financed using the amazing system that we outlined together.

The PFF system is designed to get better and better each year as long as you can maintain your level of personal responsibility. Think of it as an annual wealth-building marathon that you have to keep running. It is not a 100- or 200- meter dash to the finish line.

Because the race is a marathon, you need to understand pacing. If I believed it was a sprint, I would burst off the starting line too quickly and would not be able to finish the race at the end. But if I paced myself at the beginning, I could run the entire race.

The same is true with your new PFF system. It is not a quick sprint to the finish line, taking only one, two, or three years of funding. It is a lifetime of funding that needs to be focused on. When you follow your coach's instructions, you will see why this is so important.

If you are eager to learn, follow your coach's instructions, and keep your PFF GPS set to "always on" you will win the race and leave a legacy for your children.

Instead of investing, losing, investing, losing, sometimes winning, and then investing elsewhere, you will have a roadmap, stability, and people on your side handing you water and mini fans as you pass those checkpoints.

CHAPTER 8
THE POWER OF PFF

"If we command our wealth, we shall be rich and free. If our wealth commands us, we are poor indeed."

Edmund Burke

There is amazing power in a custom PFF system because it equips you with the tools and processes that you need to succeed financially without stripping you of control or the ability to understand what is going on with your money at any given time.

In this outrageous age of expansive investment portfolios, stocks, bonds, money markets, and real estate, it can be tough to know how best to leverage the money that you earn. With your Private Family Financing system, the ball will always be in your proverbial court.

Your Long-term Legacy

After walking my clients through everything you have just read, there is always one clear question that needs to be asked before we move any further.

"How long will I have to pay premiums, and when do they stop?"

It is a very valid question, especially since you will need to know a lot more than that to keep your finances in order. The answer is not a simple one, but it is one that is logical to justify.

Your premiums will never stop because you will want to fund and capitalize your program for life. You will be able to afford a better quality of life this way, and you will be able to pass on this lifestyle to your children when you pass away one day.

It is a long-term[25] legacy system that also happens to have a lot of excellent real-world application in finance, which is why it is gaining popularity over term insurance. When one of my clients finally realizes the real potential of a PFF system, they get very excited.

Not only will it revamp and improve their lives, but the lives of their children and grandchildren, too. Rick Warren once said, "Life is like a marathon. It is crowded at the start, but it thins out rather quickly."

When you begin your PFF knowing that it is a lifetime program that will build a legacy for future generations, you will not be tricked or taken advantage of during the process.

The REAL Difference

---

[25] How to Set and Keep Personal Financial Goals, http://www.moneymanagement.org/Budgeting-Tools/Credit-Articles/Money-and-Budgeting/How-To-Set-and-Keep-Personal-Financial-Goals.aspx

It is 2 Timothy 4:3–4 that reads, *"For the time will come when people will not put up with sound doctrine. Instead to suit their own desires, they will gather around them a great number of teachers to say what their itching ears want to hear. They will turn their ears away from the truth and turn aside to myths."*

The now perpetual and common practice of investing is destroying individual lifetime savings and retirement programs. I see it all the time—older people that have been forced to go back to work out of necessity because they did not plan well enough or, worse, their plan let them down in a big way.

When our clients are coached about the PFF system, it is the beginning of the journey to completely eliminate the chance of that ever happening to you. In this way, you have learned to practice R.E.A.L.

The individual that practices R.E.A.L. understands that they are being trained for a marathon and will not get caught up in the first part of the race—or on mile five or mile eight. When your peers seem to be ahead of you, it will not matter because you are on pace and understand your own financial strategy.

You will not get caught up in the emotional torrent and invest in fads—like the dotcom rush[26] or the real estate boom. Those things eventually crashed. Before the finish line, you know that you will pass them financially.

It is not how you start the race but how you finish it that matters. This difference is R.E.A.L:

- RECAPTURE the cost of everything that you do.
- Build EQUITY for you and your family.
- Have the funds AVAILABLE when you need them.
- When you are finished, you will be able to leave a LEGACY.

---

[26] Market Crashes: The Dotcom Crash, http://www.investopedia.com/features/crashes/crashes8.asp

You will be trained to win the gold today, tomorrow, and in the future by always knowing what is happening with your money and your own PFF system. An old Chinese proverb says that "fifty percent is the first step."

The EVA Pillar

Once you have decided to initiate your own PFF system, you will need the EVA pillar to allow R.E.A.L. to work for you and your family. EVA[27] is a fairly complex term that I have simplified for you based on a close friend's apt interpretation.

If you borrow money from a bank, when you pay them back, you have to also pay interest on the money. If you borrow from a credit card company, an insurance company, or a car dealership, you always have to pay them interest. But if you use your own money, you never pay yourself interest. Why not?

When you do not pay yourself interest, you are openly declaring that *your* money is not worth as much as other people's money. EVA in its simplest terms = paying yourself interest on your money.

Remember Proverbs 23:7 (For as he thinks in his heart, so is he)—you have been programmed to believe that your money means nothing. Changing your thinking is the first step. That way you will pay interest back to your PFF system when you do any form of financing—car, boat, vacation, it does not matter.

When R.E.A.L. is in play, it will increase your efficiency. Paying this small amount of interest over time boosts your financial wellbeing. No one has their first or second cars or the money that they paid for them. If you do not have any more money than the person that finaced your car, it does you no

---

[27] Economic Value Added and the Measurement of Financial Performance, http://finance.wharton.upenn.edu/~acmack/Chapter_12_app.pdf

good.

Recapturing money is the only way to make sure that this does not happen. Some clients insist that they pay cash because "I hate payments." It is wrong to think that by paying cash you have no payments. Do you not have to save the money you need to buy your next car? Yes!

Would you want to save that money in a regular systematic system or whenever you have the cash to put into your account? Does the mortgage company require regular systematic payments, and the car company, and the credit card company? It works for them because it works. Practicing EVA with your R.E.A.L. and PFF system works.

Adding to the Equation

At Living Wealth, we always encourage our clients to practice using the following financial equation:

EVA + R.E.A.L. + PFF = Long-term Financial Success!

Then I ask my client if they can show me a concept or strategy that will allow them to recapture all of the interest plus the principal amount that they pay on every car that they buy between now and the day that they graduate. They have no idea how to do that.

But this is exactly what I want to show you! A few people might bow out, but mostly people are open to being coached financially. I am a big sports fan as you may have discovered from my marathon, exercise, and motor sports analogies.

The sport I love the most, however, is college basketball. I realized that the coaches of college basketball have a great system and if their players buy into that system, the team often becomes unstoppable. The players that do not buy into the system sit on the bench, transfer, or eventually buy into the system down the line. Everyone is different.

The coach understands what works and that it is not random but a formalized system that guarantees that his team does better together than as individuals. My coaches adopt the same mindset and understand that R.E.A.L. + PFF can work for you and your family, even though not everyone is Michael Jordan.

Even Mike himself needed other players and his coach to succeed. Working together with your coach will result in financial, emotional, and spiritual success without working any harder than you are now. You do not have to change your cash flow, and you will never lose control over your money with the R.E.A.L. + PFF system.

I had never heard about EVA[28] until about 13 years ago. Paying yourself interest was a foreign concept to me, and I already felt pretty good about my finances after paying cash for all of my cars since the mid '80s. I was then shown about EVA and how I could use my life insurance policies to finance everything I was doing at home and in business.

Outlining the Impact

I had been in life insurance for some 30 years already and was a Chartered Life Underwriter and Chartered Financial Consultant after many hours of testing and studying and a wealth of costs, energy, and resources. No one had ever told me about using my own policies.

I was fairly upset at discovering what my own policies and EVA could have done for me and began something of a rampage trying to find out who else knew about this revolutionary tool. Not once in 30 years had anyone told me to pay myself interest. Not once did anyone tell me that I could use my life insurance

---

[28] Israel Shaked, Creating Value Through E.V.A. – Myth or Reality?, http://www.strategy-business.com/article/12756?gko=05fdd

policies as collateral to buy a car, and I had five drivers in the family, so I had purchased a lot of vehicles at that time.

After I read R. Nelson Nash's book *Becoming Your Own Banker,* only then did I realize that finance is a process and not a product. I owned the product, my DPWL, but I did not know the process. The impact of this was huge.

I was studying one evening and brushing up on private financing when the penny finally dropped. I got a clear picture of how to relate to this process I had been lacking. In 1978 I had bought my first computer—before Windows or Apple even existed and before even DOS was created, I believe.

In 1992 I met with a specific individual. While going through a presentation, this person told me to hold down alt and tab at the same time. I was shocked. All the programs I had loaded on my computer were still there. I thought they had vanished and had loaded the same program three times during the presentation.

At this time, I understood that while I owned the product (the computer), I did not yet understand its processes. I remember thanking the person, saying, "I do not care if you buy anything or not. I am just glad you showed me how to use this computer. It will save me hours of time in the future."

Perfecting the Process

Processes, you see, matter. As I read *Becoming Your Own Banker,* I realized that I had owned life insurance for over 30 years and had never fully understood the process for it. That was a great day when the truth was revealed to me.

I began to realize the full power of the product (my DPWL) and the process of using it to benefit me, my family, and all of my past and future clients. Anyone can have life insurance and pay monthly premiums into an account that stands stagnant.

It is when you empower yourself to understand how that product can be used through the right processes, you can discover a new world of possibility. Perfecting the process is still a concern of mine, and I am still a member of a number of study groups within the life insurance industry.

The moment my proverbial penny had dropped, I began telling everyone about my discovery. At first, it was a strange thing. Then it became my normal. As I slowly spread the truth with other life insurance professionals—many of whom had been in the business for longer than I had—I realized that no one knew about it.

Somewhere along the line, the power of the process had been lost. The process of our products had been around for more than 200 years, yet they were completely hidden from everyone that used them.

It was at that defining moment that I realized the mission for my life, until the day I graduate (go to be with the LORD), would be to coach individuals, families, and agents on the miraculous processes in finance and how to incorporate the PFF system into every family. The fundamental truth is so valuable to your family and your family's legacy that it will allow each consecutive generation to gain in wealth over time.

The only thing that needs to remain constant is the coaching. Everyone needs a coach to look out for those technical aspects and to make sure that their clients are practicing the three rules of PFF in their own lives.

God often gives us enlightening moments where we can either choose to follow a new path or ignore it and continue along our way. At that time, I knew I was forging a new path and that it would be tough, but I had to show people how to make the most of their PFF system.

CHAPTER 9
THE LOAN RANGER ARRIVES

"If you've got a dollar and you spend 29 cents on a loaf of bread, you've got 71 cents left; but if you've got seventeen grand and you spend 29 cents on a loaf of bread, you've still got seventeen grand. There's a math lesson for you."

Steve Martin

The middle-class hates borrowing (which is a loan) money, but it is something that they have to do in order to survive in a debt system like we have today. What if you could borrow money and then recover it later on? Would that change the way you viewed financial possibilities? Of course it would.

The next step in this process is taking out a loan from the insurance company using your PFF system. See illustration 1 for a graphic representation of this step.

Private Family Financing: Illustration 1
$70k Policy premiums paid over 7 years with car loans year 3 and no retirement

Policy Year	Age	Premium	Car Loan Payments	Car Purchases	Cash Value in PFF Account	Death Benefit
1	26	$10,000			$5,873	$680,939
2	27	$10,000			$12,215	$722,984
3	28	$10,000	$6,000	$25,000	$4,203	$751,743
4	29	$10,000	$6,000		$18,653	$798,212
5	30	$10,000	$6,000		$34,079	$844,445
6	31	$10,000	$6,000		$50,472	$890,922
7	32	$10,000	$6,000		$67,881	$937,742
Total Premium & Loan Repaid:			**$100,000**		**Cash Value Growth:**	**$67,881**
8	33		$6,000	$25,000	$51,521	$904,368
9	34		$6,000		$60,669	$897,298
10	35		$6,000		$70,346	$891,530
11	36		$6,000		$80,603	$887,071
12	37		$6,000		$91,473	$884,079
Total Loan Repaid:			**$30,000**		**Cash Value Growth:**	**$23,592**
13	38		$6,000	$25,000	$76,541	$855,967
14	39		$6,000		$87,240	$854,189
15	40		$6,000		$98,600	$853,735
16	41		$6,000		$110,663	$854,589
17	42		$6,000		$123,478	$856,766
Total Loan Repaid:			**$30,000**		**Cash Value Growth:**	**$32,005**
18	43		$6,000	$25,000	$110,640	$833,871
19	44		$6,000		$123,551	$837,303
20	45		$6,000		$137,261	$842,051
21	46		$6,000		$151,810	$848,157
22	47		$6,000		$167,240	$855,608
Total Loan Repaid:			**$30,000**		**Cash Value Growth:**	**$43,762**
23	48		$6,000	$25,000	$157,125	$837,993
24	49		$6,000		$172,892	$846,689
25	50		$6,000		$189,582	$856,701
26	51		$6,000		$207,224	$868,072
27	52		$6,000		$225,849	$880,746
Total Loan Repaid:			**$30,000**		**Cash Value Growth:**	**$58,609**
28	53		$6,000	$25,000	$219,051	$868,245
29	54		$6,000		$238,221	$881,980
30	55		$6,000		$258,403	$896,902

Details:	Automobile Cost:
Female age 25; preferred	$25,000 every 5 years; years 3 to 48
$4,000 base; $6,000 PUA yr 1-7	Loan: 7.420095% for 5 years
Repaid loans to PFF years 3-52	Annual Loan Payment: $6,000
	Year 3 Loan used Policy and Commercial Bank

Private Family Financing: Illustration 1
$70k Policy premiums paid over 7 years with car loans year 3 and no retirement

Policy Year	Age	Premium	Car Loan Payments	Car Purchases	Cash Value in PFF Account	Death Benefit
31	56		$6,000		$279,688	$912,974
32	57		$6,000		$302,124	$930,357
Total Loan Repaid: $30,000				**Cash Value Growth: $76,275**		
33	58		$6,000	$25,000	$299,325	$922,636
34	59		$6,000		$322,722	$941,208
35	60		$6,000		$347,390	$961,103
36	61		$6,000		$373,404	$982,304
37	62		$6,000		$400,841	$1,004,837
Total Loan Repaid: $30,000				**Cash Value Growth: $98,717**		
38	63		$6,000	$25,000	$403,315	$1,002,292
39	64		$6,000		$432,275	$1,026,045
40	65		$6,000		$462,807	$1,051,137
41	66		$6,000		$494,981	$1,077,609
42	67		$6,000		$528,887	$1,105,511
Total Loan Repaid: $30,000				**Cash Value Growth: $128,046**		
43	68		$6,000	$25,000	$538,151	$1,108,423
44	69		$6,000		$574,222	$1,137,791
45	70		$6,000		$612,190	$1,168,664
46	71		$6,000		$652,132	$1,201,085
47	72		$6,000		$694,130	$1,235,129
Total Loan Repaid: $30,000				**Cash Value Growth: $165,243**		
48	73		$6,000	$25,000	$711,815	$1,244,466
49	74		$6,000		$756,654	$1,280,528
50	75		$6,000		$803,736	$1,318,375
51	76		$6,000		$853,163	$1,358,086
52	77		$6,000		$905,035	$1,399,708
Total Loan Repaid: $30,000				**Cash Value Growth: $210,905**		
53	78				$953,114	$1,436,773
54	79				$1,003,488	$1,475,562
55	80				$1,056,249	$1,516,115
56	81				$1,111,518	$1,558,497
57	82				$1,169,093	$1,602,770
58	83				$1,229,003	$1,649,383
59	84				$1,291,441	$1,698,440
60	85				$1,356,484	$1,749,875

		Total Outlay		Total Car Purchases
Totals:		$370,000		-$250,000
		Net Cost:	$120,000	

The Next Step Is a Loan?

Take out a loan.[29] In this example, you are still capitalizing your policy, and it is time for a newer car. You will get a loan from your insurance company and a conventional bank for $25,000, taken in the third year.

Your payments will be $500 every month for sixty months. That means your total payments will amount to $30,000. In effect, this means that you will pay $25,000 in principal and $5,000 in interest.

You will allow for PFF (because you will pay yourself interest), and R.E.A.L. will work for you too, to begin the process that breaks the bonds of financial slavery.

Every five years you will continue to buy a new $25,000 car. Now comes the magic part, the part that has made me wealthy through car financing. It begins with a loan—and ends in something so much more valuable!

Recovering Costs the Smart Way

The time has come to be a loan ranger! When financing your first car while you are still capitalizing your program, you will be able to recover 91% of your costs.[30]

Let me explain how I arrive at 91%:

$ 70,000 premium

+ $ 30,000 loan repayments

_____

$100,000

-$ 25,000 cost of car

_____

[29] What Is a Loan?, http://www.usnews.com/education/best-colleges/paying-for-college/student-loan/articles/2010/10/08/what-is-a-loan

[30] Cost Recovery, http://financial-dictionary.thefreedictionary.com/cost+recovery

$ 75,000
$ 67,881 your PFF cash value
÷ $ 75,000

91% = 91 cents on every dollar

That means that you can recapture 91 cents on every dollar that you spend. I have never met anyone that has not answered YES to this question:

"How would you like to get 91 cents of every dollar back that you spend on cars?"

Most people would do that all day long! When you finance your second car, the process is exactly the same as with your first one, only you are no longer capitalizing your PFF program.

Recaptured	$25,000	principal
	$23,592	increased value
	$48,592	total

$48,592 ÷ $30,000 amount of payments = $1.62 for each dollar in payments.

This way, you will borrow $25,000 and pay back $500 a month for 60 months, for a total of $30,000. Easy, just the same as last time. Only now you are recapturing $1.62 for every dollar that you have spent.

At this point you are recapturing your principal plus your interest, and R.E.A.L. is really starting to work for you and your family. The bonds of financial slavery are finally starting to break in a noticeable fashion!

Is This REAL Enough?

Here is how I managed to achieve this:

- You RECAPTURED principal plus interest and an additional $18,592.
- EQUITY in your PFF, which is now $91,473.
- AVAILABLE to use as you wish.
- LEGACY of $884,000 that will go to those you love if you pass away.

All of this just from buying cars that you would be purchasing anyway.

The PFF program gets better with the financing of each additional car. In this example, when you finally finance your third car, you will recapture $1.90 for each dollar that you spend, and it improves as you buy more vehicles.

By the time you finance your tenth car, you will recapture $7.00 for every dollar that you spend, and your PFF system and R.E.A.L. will be paving the road to financial freedom for you.

At this point (after financing the 10th car) you will enjoy the following:

- RECAPTURED principal plus interest and add on another $200,905.
- EQUITY in your PFF, which has grown to $905,035.
- AVAILABLE for your retirement, charitable giving, taxes, mortgages, etc.
- LEGACY in the program amounts to $1,399,000.

This is just one policy, but if you listen to your coach through your lifetime—while your coach increases your workouts—it is likely that you will have many policies, along with your children and their children too.

Life Insurance and the PFF System

This example is just for one car in the family.

What would happen if you did two, three, four, or five cars?

A small fortune has been removed from my legacy because no one had told me about using my own life insurance along with a PFF system.

Moving from illustration one (1) to illustration two (2) is the next step. It is time to show you how and why your route should change.

The Marathon Reminder

In illustration two, there are two cars that were bought in year three and every five years after that while capitalizing this program at $20,000 per year for seven years.

The two changes to the PFF are annual capitalization from $10,000/yr to $20,000/yr. Total monthly payments change from $500 a month to $1,000 a month for both cars for 60 months.

This could be two cars at $25,000, three cars for $50,000 or just one car. Most families today have two drivers or more, and your PFF plan has to be flexible for payments and premiums.

The PFF Program and R.E.A.L. need to be looked at after financing cars in year eight.

- RECAPITALIZE principal plus interest and an additional $37,917.
- EQUITY of $184,134.
- AVAILABLE for use whenever you desire it.
- LEGACY of $1,785,135.

Recaptured	$50,000	principal
	$47,917	increase in value
	$97.917	total

$97,917 ÷ $60,000 amount of payments = $1.63 for every dollar of payments.

By the tenth (10) car this amounts to over $7.97 for every dollar of payments.

Private Family Financing: Illustration 2

$140k Policy premiums paid over 7 years with car loans year 3 and no retirement

Policy Year	Age	Premium	Car Loan Payments	Car Purchases	Cash Value in PFF Account	Death Benefit
1	26	$20,000			$11,745	$1,378,246
2	27	$20,000			$24,433	$1,462,335
3	28	$20,000	$12,000	$50,000	$8,412	$1,519,876
4	29	$20,000	$12,000		$37,414	$1,612,838
5	30	$20,000	$12,000		$68,376	$1,705,327
6	31	$20,000	$12,000		$101,277	$1,798,313
7	32	$20,000	$12,000		$136,217	$1,891,999
Total Premium & Loan Repaid:			**$200,000**		**Cash Value Growth:**	**$136,217**
8	33		$12,000	$50,000	$103,628	$1,825,311
9	34		$12,000		$122,062	$1,811,248
10	35		$12,000		$141,560	$1,799,802
11	36		$12,000		$162,229	$1,790,992
12	37		$12,000		$184,134	$1,785,135
Total Loan Repaid:			**$60,000**		**Cash Value Growth:**	**$47,917**
13	38		$12,000	$50,000	$154,444	$1,729,054
14	39		$12,000		$176,027	$1,725,658
15	40		$12,000		$198,944	$1,724,932
16	41		$12,000		$223,279	$1,726,839
17	42		$12,000		$249,132	$1,731,410
Total Loan Repaid:			**$60,000**		**Cash Value Growth:**	**$64,998**
18	43		$12,000	$50,000	$223,692	$1,685,857
19	44		$12,000		$249,767	$1,692,977
20	45		$12,000		$277,454	$1,702,752
21	46		$12,000		$306,838	$1,715,263
22	47		$12,000		$338,001	$1,730,485
Total Loan Repaid:			**$60,000**		**Cash Value Growth:**	**$88,869**
23	48		$12,000	$50,000	$318,092	$1,695,597
24	49		$12,000		$349,966	$1,713,354
25	50		$12,000		$383,707	$1,733,766
26	51		$12,000		$419,372	$1,756,920
27	52		$12,000		$457,024	$1,782,702
Total Loan Repaid:			**$60,000**		**Cash Value Growth:**	**$119,023**
28	53		$12,000	$50,000	$443,853	$1,758,155
29	54		$12,000		$482,640	$1,786,103
30	55		$12,000		$523,475	$1,816,446

Details:	Automobile Cost:
Female age 25; preferred	$50,000 every 5 years; years 3 to 48
$8,000 base; $12,000 PUA yr 1-7	Loan: 7.420095% for 5 years
Repaid loans to PFF years 3-52	Annual Loan Payment: $12,000
	Year 3 Loan used Policy and Commercial Bank

Private Family Financing: Illustration 2
$140k Policy premiums paid over 7 years with car loans year 3 and no retirement

Policy Year	Age	Premium	Car Loan Payments	Car Purchases	Cash Value in PFF Account	Death Benefit
31	56		$12,000		$566,544	$1,849,110
32	57		$12,000		$611,939	$1,884,422
		Total Loan Repaid:	**$60,000**		**Cash Value Growth:**	**$154,915**
33	58		$12,000	$50,000	$606,894	$1,869,550
34	59		$12,000		$654,269	$1,907,289
35	60		$12,000		$704,218	$1,947,704
36	61		$12,000		$756,895	$1,990,755
37	62		$12,000		$812,451	$2,036,499
		Total Loan Repaid:	**$60,000**		**Cash Value Growth:**	**$200,512**
38	63		$12,000	$50,000	$818,119	$2,032,113
39	64		$12,000		$876,797	$2,080,353
40	65		$12,000		$938,658	$2,131,299
41	66		$12,000		$1,003,850	$2,185,036
42	67		$12,000		$1,072,549	$2,241,663
		Total Loan Repaid:	**$60,000**		**Cash Value Growth:**	**$260,098**
43	68		$12,000	$50,000	$1,092,012	$2,248,342
44	69		$12,000		$1,165,137	$2,307,969
45	70		$12,000		$1,242,107	$2,370,639
46	71		$12,000		$1,323,081	$2,436,442
47	72		$12,000		$1,408,222	$2,505,530
		Total Loan Repaid:	**$60,000**		**Cash Value Growth:**	**$335,673**
48	73		$12,000	$50,000	$1,444,793	$2,525,245
49	74		$12,000		$1,535,735	$2,598,453
50	75		$12,000		$1,631,224	$2,675,274
51	76		$12,000		$1,731,468	$2,755,873
52	77		$12,000		$1,836,672	$2,840,340
		Total Loan Repaid:	**$60,000**		**Cash Value Growth:**	**$428,450**
53	78				$1,934,360	$2,915,743
54	79				$2,036,713	$2,994,647
55	80				$2,143,918	$3,077,132
56	81				$2,256,218	$3,163,330
57	82				$2,373,205	$3,253,370
58	83				$2,494,939	$3,348,160
59	84				$2,621,811	$3,447,913
60	85				$2,753,979	$3,552,498

		Total Outlay		Total Car Purchases
Totals:		$740,000		-$500,000
		Net Cost:	**$240,000**	

This does not take inflation or anything like that into account. So yes!—it is totally possible to break out of financial bondage and to have dreams and visions that *can* be fulfilled and passed on to the next generation.

Nothing fancy has been done here. The individual you see is working like they always have; they have not changed their cash flow or have taken any risks at all that have placed their capital in danger. As time goes by, it is the marathon that wins.

The Defining Difference: Systems

You might say—"I am not 26. How is this system going to help me at all?"

The good news is that this system does not only work for youngsters, it works for older people as well. Anyone at any age can benefit from this system. The oldest client I have worked with is 86 and he wanted to purchase at least one truck and recapture the principal and interest. He has purchased three trucks and two cars for his wife.

It is important to remember that regardless of your age, it is still a marathon, not a sprint.

Now, let me ask you a question: "Do you believe the car you are driving now will be the last one you ever get to buy?"

If the answer is yes, I have news for you.

PFF is a generational thing.

One of your children or grandchildren will be able to buy a car using this system, and they will benefit from the process. You and your entire family can benefit if you take the time to look into what makes the PFF system so incredible.

Leaving a legacy is one of the most important parts of growing old. The next generation of your family will be able to do so much more because of your keen insight into the world of financial decision-making when you hand over the reins.

CHAPTER 10
CHEATING THE SYSTEM

"To be healthy, wealthy, happy and successful
in any and all areas of your life you need to be
aware that you need to think healthy, wealthy,
happy and successful thoughts twenty four hours
a day and cancel all negative, destructive,
fearful and unhappy thoughts. These two types of
thought cannot coexist if you want to share in the
abundance that surrounds us all."

Sidney Madwed

There are not many people that know about Private Family
Financing and the systems that we use to gain you wealth
during your lifetime. It is something that I had to figure out for
myself after facing some uncomfortable questions.

You can think of it as a way to cheat the system that is
cheating you. This is the best way to seize back your financial
freedom and enjoy a life of abundance, the kind God wants you
to have all throughout your life.

The Little Known Cheat

It is true that even a 50-year-old can benefit from the PFF system. You can see here in illustration three (3) how it works.

Here a 50-year-old person finances a car with his PFF system in year three, while he is still capitalizing his policy.

He finances a $50,000 car for $1,000 per month for 60 months. He has recaptured on his very first car a figure of 99 cents for every dollar spent.

$210,000   total of premium + car payments years 1-7
$ 50,000   cash price of the car
$160,000   net cost of car
Cash value of PFF = $159,185 ÷ $160,000 = .99 so you received 99 cents of each dollar on the very first car.

Then the PFF helps the coach show the client his progress that he makes with the car financing—for himself or a family member once every five years.

The dollars that would have left the family are now staying in the family and can be recycled the same way a financing company would do it. You have become your own bank!

This amounts to hundreds of thousands of dollars and possibly even millions for most families. When the patriarch or matriarch is 73 (my own mother purchased her last car at 74), they will finance the car for fifty thousand dollars.

The payments are $1,000 per month for 60 months.

- RECAPTURED all of the principal and interest plus additional $88,852.
- EQUITY of $445,060.
- AVAILABLE whenever you need it.
- LEGACY amounts to $695,491.

Private Family Financing: Illustration 3
$150k Policy premiums paid over 7 years with car loans year 3 and no retirement

Policy Year	Age	Premium	Car Loan Payments	Car Purchases	Cash Value in PFF Account	Death Benefit
1	51	$30,000			$21,382	$474,065
2	52	$20,000			$34,764	$506,158
3	53	$20,000	$12,000	$50,000	$16,284	$499,246
4	54	$20,000	$12,000		$49,317	$542,688
5	55	$20,000	$12,000		$84,067	$586,573
6	56	$20,000	$12,000		$120,648	$631,407
7	57	$20,000	$12,000		$159,185	$677,388
Total Premium & Loan Repaid:			**$210,000**	**Cash Value Growth:**	**$159,185**	
8	58		$12,000	$50,000	$126,776	$628,078
9	59		$12,000		$145,307	$630,195
10	60		$12,000		$164,850	$633,661
11	61		$12,000		$185,451	$638,563
12	62		$12,000		$207,162	$644,991
Total Loan Repaid:			**$60,000**	**Cash Value Growth:**	**$47,977**	
13	63		$12,000	$50,000	$177,110	$600,174
14	64		$12,000		$198,097	$606,948
15	65		$12,000		$220,197	$615,370
16	66		$12,000		$243,477	$625,436
17	67		$12,000		$268,018	$637,164
Total Loan Repaid:			**$60,000**	**Cash Value Growth:**	**$60,856**	
18	68		$12,000	$50,000	$241,005	$597,615
19	69		$12,000		$265,244	$609,514
20	70		$12,000		$290,832	$622,886
21	71		$12,000		$317,801	$637,723
22	72		$12,000		$346,208	$654,103
Total Loan Repaid:			**$60,000**	**Cash Value Growth:**	**$78,190**	
23	73		$12,000	$50,000	$323,146	$619,162
24	74		$12,000		$351,425	$635,847

Details:	Automobile Cost:
Male age 50; preferred	$50,000 every 5 years; years 3 to 23
$8,000 base; $12,000 PUA yr 1-7	Loan: 7.420095% for 5 years
$10,000 1035 exchange year 1;	Annual Loan Payment: $12,000
Repaid loans to PFF years 3-27	

Private Family Financing: Illustration 3

$150k Policy premiums paid over 7 years with car loans year 3 and no retirement

Policy Year	Age	Premium	Car Loan Payments	Car Purchases	Cash Value in PFF Account	Death Benefit
25	75		$12,000		$381,126	$654,122
26	76		$12,000		$412,313	$673,988
27	77		$12,000		$445,060	$695,491
Total Loan Repaid: $60,000				**Cash Value Growth: $98,852**		
28	78				$466,702	$705,686
29	79				$489,222	$716,937
30	80				$512,605	$729,303
31	81				$536,887	$742,855
32	82				$562,069	$757,621
33	83				$588,206	$773,680
34	84				$615,349	$790,973
35	85				$643,504	$809,508
36	86				$672,670	$829,329
37	87				$702,833	$850,515
38	88				$733,986	$873,142
39	89				$766,147	$897,269
40	90				**$799,329**	**$922,951**

		Total Outlay		Total Car Purchases
Totals:		$450,000		-$250,000
	Net Cost:	$200,000		

Capitalizing on Your Policy

Finally, in illustration four (4), you can see how this very same program is used for retirement income. Your coach from Living Wealth will demonstrate the flexibility and versatility of your PFF program while they put you through some serious financial workouts.

In this illustration, a woman at age 90 has withdrawn more dollars than she has put into the program while still leaving a legacy of over half-a-million dollars.

How is this possible, you may ask! What crazy financial wizardry is going on?

None at all! These numbers are straightforward and show exactly how the system works. We have used it to make ourselves wealthy, and we use it to do the same for our clients.

To capitalize on this policy, you must first understand how it works. This book has provided you with some excellent insight into the world of Private Family Financing, R.E.A.L., and EVA pillars, and they work to remove you from the financial rat-race.

You do not have to spend the rest of your life in poverty, wondering where all of your money has gone. With this easy PFF system, nothing changes except your mindset and the status of your wealth and wellbeing.

Using PFF in Retirement

It is true that PFF can be used in retirement to supplement the ever-plummeting pension levels and the mess that Medicaid and Medicare have made for pensioners in America.

The truth is that people reaching retirement age have few options—but PFF is definitely one of them. I wish I could tell everyone in the world how it works so that they can repair the damage that our corrupt system has caused.

Private Family Financing: Illustration 4
$150k Policy premiums paid over 7 years with car loans year 3 and with retirement

Policy Year	Age	Premium	Car Loan Payments	Car Purchases	Cash Value in PFF Account	Death Benefit
1	51	$30,000			$21,382	$474,065
2	52	$20,000			$34,764	$506,158
3	53	$20,000	$12,000	$50,000	$16,284	$499,246
4	54	$20,000	$12,000		$49,317	$542,688
5	55	$20,000	$12,000		$84,067	$586,573
6	56	$20,000	$12,000		$120,648	$631,407
7	57	$20,000	$12,000		$159,185	$677,388
Total Premium & Loan Repaid:			**$210,000**	**Cash Value Growth:**		**$159,185**
8	58		$12,000	$50,000	$126,776	$628,078
9	59		$12,000		$145,307	$630,195
10	60		$12,000		$164,850	$633,661
11	61		$12,000		$185,451	$638,563
12	62		$12,000		$207,162	$644,991
Total Loan Repaid:			**$60,000**	**Cash Value Growth:**		**$47,977**
13	63		$12,000	$50,000	$177,110	$600,174
14	64		$12,000		$198,097	$606,948
15	65		$12,000		$220,197	$615,370
16	66		$12,000		$243,477	$625,436
17	67		$12,000		$268,018	$637,164
Total Loan Repaid:			**$60,000**	**Cash Value Growth:**		**$60,856**
18	68		$12,000	$50,000	$241,005	$597,615
19	69		$12,000		$265,244	$609,514
20	70		$12,000		$290,832	$622,886
21	71		$12,000		$317,801	$637,723
22	72		$12,000		$346,208	$654,103
Total Loan Repaid:			**$60,000**	**Cash Value Growth:**		**$78,190**
23	73		$12,000	$50,000	$323,146	$619,162
24	74		$12,000		$351,425	$635,847

Details:	Automobile Cost:
Male age 50; preferred	$50,000 every 5 years; years 3 to 23
$8,000 base; $12,000 PUA yr 1-7	Loan: 7.420095% for 5 years
$10,000 1035 exchange year 1;	Annual Loan Payment: $12,000
Repaid loans to PFF years 3-27	
Withdraw $15,000 retirement age 75-90	

Private Family Financing: Illustration 4
$150k Policy premiums paid over 7 years with car loans year 3 and with retirement

Policy Year	Age	Premium	Car Loan Payments	Car Purchases	Cash Value in PFF Account	Death Benefit
25	75	-$15,000	$12,000		$365,327	$631,902
26	76	-$15,000	$12,000		$379,882	$629,319
27	77	-$15,000	$12,000		$395,125	$628,099
28	78	-$15,000			$398,359	$615,254
29	79	-$15,000			$401,533	$603,099
30	80	-$15,000			$404,603	$591,635
31	81	-$15,000			$407,567	$580,866
32	82	-$15,000			$410,398	$570,760
33	83	-$15,000			$413,111	$561,322
34	84	-$15,000			$415,714	$552,447
35	85	-$15,000			$418,178	$544,091
36	86	-$15,000			$420,477	$536,227
37	87	-$15,000			$422,566	$528,859
38	88	-$15,000			$424,418	$521,979
39	89	-$15,000			$426,022	$515,570
40	90	-$15,000			$427,359	$509,605

		Total Outlay	Total Retire Income	Total Car Purchases
Totals:		$450,000	-$240,000	-$250,000
	Net Cost:	-$40,000		
	Recovered entire cost plus death benefit to family			

Recent statistics indicate that more than 65%[31] of retirees are seeing cost of living expenses rise, with only 48% of people able to retire at their projected age.

Unfortunately, people are being forced to retire at later and later ages, which is just not good for anyone in the long run. A Private Family Financing system can transform the way that you save and the lifestyle that you can afford to live.

All you have to do is approach one of our excellent coaches at Living Wealth and ask for assistance. We will educate you— not once, but consistently—through this process, and you will see how well it works after you get to reclaim the money you have spent on your first car bought using this amazing method.

Imagine being able to buy a car for each of your kids, for yourself and another loved one—and earn money while doing it! That is the dream, is it not?

The Only Route to Happiness

I was once where you are—working hard, paying the bills, and saving as much as I could, although intermittently. Looking back, those savings were never actual savings; they were just pipe-dreams.

I would often have to dip into them to get us out of a spot or to solve a family problem on the fly. That is no way to live! Your savings should be something that you can watch grow over time and that you can improve with careful planning and a good finance coach.

It became clear to me back then that the only route to happiness was to find a way out of the rat-race and away from the ever-mounting debt and struggle I was living in. I did this by trusting God and following my heart.

---

[31] Robert Laura, These Retirement Stats Paint a Troubling Picture, http://www.fa-mag.com/news/these-retirement-stats-paints-a-troubling-picture-16493.html

I truly believe that this is your opportunity to do the same thing.

You know how every now and then it feels as though the universe is trying to tell you something? Well, if you have been struggling for most of your life—searching for a way out—then this is it.

There are no tricks with this system. The great thing is that you get to regain control of the money that you earn. You finally get to keep it and spend it on life experiences that you genuinely want to have.

The only route to happiness is realizing that the system is broken. It is not you; it is the system. So, time for a new system?

Your Financial Recovery

Recovering from debt is difficult, but the best news is that when you partner with a financial coach that cares, there is no debt mountain too steep.

In fact, our financial coaches relish the challenge. No matter how deep you are or how much trouble you have found yourself in, we can help. Recovering includes wiping out your debt and revamping your finances so that the debt system works *for* you, not against you.

You will transition from someone that lives to work to someone that works to live. The difference is subtle, but money is the partition that divides the two. No one can be happy when they are broke and when they know that they have not done their best at sorting out their financial situation.

The future is uncertain, and with this in mind, the only buffer between you and the impossibility in the world is God and the abundance you stand to gain in this life. If you work very hard, you should be able to enjoy your money.

It is not a sin to want some financial freedom. Take control of your debt, of your existing policies, and of the outdated methods of managing them. Please, do not trust someone with your money.

There is a vast chasm between giving your money away and partnering with someone to help you manage your own money. The old system of "non-responsibility" does not work for anyone anymore—the risks are simply too high.

If you do not believe me, look at your own finances! Look at the finances of close friends who have done everything "right" and still cannot go away on vacation because they are crippled by debt.

This is your financial recovery. This is the beginning of your journey to financial freedom.[32]

On the Road to Riches

Having some spare cash does not make you rich. Paying money into a few policies does not make you rich, if those policies are treated as financial products without any kind of process attached to them.

I believe you are on the road to riches from this moment.

You have recognized that there is something "not quite right" with the world and have taken steps to counteract this inevitable truth. Your faith has brought you to Living Wealth, and you have almost finished reading this introductory book.

Now all that stands between you and using car financing to build yourself wealth and happiness is you. The most common problem that I encounter is the attitudes of some clients that refuse to believe they have been mistreating their money.

---

[32] Kim Kiyosaki, What Is Financial Freedom?, http://www.richdad.com/Resources/Rich-Dad- Financial-Education-Blog/January-2012/What-is-Financial-Freedom.aspx

Believe me, I understand. I was a qualified finance guy who was ultra-careful with money before I ever came across these principles and felt compelled to improve things for myself. I have my uncle to thank for that, but I am paying it forward as best I can.

The road to riches is also a very narrow road. It is not for everyone, and I doubt that everyone can stand to work hard on their finances, be coached, and listen to their coach when it matters. People have opinions about everything, and money is a sore point.

Never forget, however, that Private Family Financing works beyond all of that. It operates outside of the system, flipping it on its head and using what currently exists to benefit you financially.

Every time you buy a car, you get a little richer.

I would sign my name to that any day.

CONCLUSION

Thank you for reading this book and for coming with me on my journey to communicate the PFF system to you. I hope that I have done enough to convince you of the benefits of using this incredible system—the very same one that changed my life.

Not only did it change my life but the lives of my partners and coaches too. We all use it! I bet there are not many financial institutions in the world that can say that. But this is the end of the book and the beginning of your own financial journey.

You can choose to be inspired and investigate the PFF system a little more.

OR

You can choose to close this book, forget about it, and continue on the hamster wheel.

I urge you to stop to think about the next action that you perform. Life does not happen in straight lines or perfect circles. If you do click away or close this book without taking action, you may never adopt the PFF system and secure yourself financially.

This is the moment when it needs to happen.

Matthew 25:29 says, "For to everyone who has will more be given, and he will have an abundance. But from the one who has not, even what he has will be taken away."

Let this be the time that you strike out in search of answers, even if it means going to someone else for financial advice or help. My goal is not to sell you something but to genuinely inspire change—because that is the gift I have been given.

I believe that I can help you, but if I cannot, please do not end your search here. God wants you to enjoy this life and to be financially stable—of that I am certain! Go now in good faith and make real decisions about your financial future, because it matters.

God Bless,

Raymond C Petty

REFERENCES

Chapter 1

Berger, Robert, *Top 100 Money Quotes Of All Time,*
http://www.forbes.com/sites/robertberger/2014/04/30/top-100-money-quotes-of-all-time/

Chapter 2

Berger, Robert, *Top 100 Money Quotes Of All Time,*
http://www.forbes.com/sites/robertberger/2014/04/30/top-100-money-quotes-of-all-time/

Bogle, John, C, *America's Financial System – Powerful But Flawed,* http://johncbogle.com/wordpress/wp-content/uploads/2006/02/Phi-Beta-Kappa-11-2-10.pdf

Understanding Money 101,
http://www.understandingmoney101.com

Sickler, Melvin, *America's Greatest Problem – It's Debt Money System,*   http://www.rense.com/general75/amde.htm

Summary on How Money and the Monetary System Work, http://www.matrixwissen.de/index.php?option = com_content& view = article&id = 898:introductary-summary-on-how-money-and-the-monetary-system-work-en&catid = 236&lang = en&Itemid = 82

Chapter 3

Berger, Robert, *Top 100 Money Quotes Of All Time*,
http://www.forbes.com/sites/robertberger/2014/04/30/top-100-money-quotes-of-all-time/

Torrieri, Marisa, *Are You Paying Yourself First? The Money Habit That Can Boost Wealth*,
http://www.forbes.com/sites/learnvest/2014/07/24/are-you-paying-yourself-first-the-money-habit-that-can-boost-wealth/

Understanding Economic Value Added,
http://www.investopedia.com/university/eva/

Kirchhoff, Herb, *How Does Compound Interest Help You Save For Retirement?* http://finance.zacks.com/compound-interest-save-retirement-2698.html

Chapter 4

Wealth Quotes,
http://www.brainyquote.com/quotes/keywords/wealth.html

The Number One Tool Of Financial Enslavement,
http://theeconomiccollapseblog.com/archives/tag/financial-enslavement

Haden, Jeff, *The Only Way To Get Really, Really Rich*,
http://www.inc.com/jeff-haden/the-only-way-to-get-really-really-rich.html

Woodruff, Mandi, *21 Ways Rich People Think Differently*,
http://www.businessinsider.com/how-rich-people-think-differently-from-the-poor-2012-8?op = 1

Abundant Life,
http://www.openbible.info/topics/abundant_life

6 Facts You Have To Face If You Want To Be Rich,
http://www.huffingtonpost.com/wise-bread/6-facts-you-have-to-face-_b_4380802.html

Chapter 5

Wealth Quotes,
http://www.brainyquote.com/quotes/keywords/wealth.html

What Is Dividend Paying Whole Life Insurance,
http://www.bankonyourself.com/what-is-dividend-paying-whole-life-insurance

What Are Paid Up Additions,
htpp://www.becomingyourownbank.com/infinite-banking-what-are-paid-up-additions/

Holsopple, Scott, *The Importance Of Financial Literacy,*
http://www.fool.com/retirement/general/2014/08/28/the-importance-of-financial-literacy.aspx

Scism, Leslie, *Life Policies: The Whole Truth,*
http://online.wsj.com/articles/SB10001424052702303296604577450313299530278

Chapter 6

Wealth Quotes,
http://www.brainyquote.com/quotes/keywords/wealth_2.html

Sprint Cup Series Drivers Jeff Gordon,
http://www.nascar.com/en_us/sprint-cup-series/drivers/jeff-gordon.html
Leimberg, Stephan, R, Doyle, Robert, J, Jr., Buck, Keith, A, *10 Things To Know About Whole Life Insurance,*
http://www.lifehealthpro.com/2014/09/15/10-things-to-know-about-whole-life-insurance

Infinite Banking Institute,
http://www.infinitebanking.org/finder/

Chapter 7

Money And Wealth Quotes,
http://www.behappy101.com/money-and-wealth-quotes.html

Brodock, Kate, *Financial Know-How Is Important For Both Personal And Professional Success*, http://www.forbes.com/sites/katebrodock/2014/01/26/financial-know-how-is-important-for-both-personal-and-professional-success/

Sridhar Ramamoorti, The Benefits Of Continuous Monitoring, http://raw.rutgers.edu/docs/wcars/23wcars/presentations/Mike%20Cangemi-The_Benefits_of_Continuous_Monitoring_edited_final_8-11[1].pdf

Proverbs 23:7, https://www.biblegateway.com/passage/?search = Proverbs%2023:7

Kitchen Table Finances: New Survey Reveals Increased Personal Financial Responsibility Among Americans with Goals to Save More and Reduce Debt, http://www.newyorklife.com/about/kitchen-table-finances-new-survey-reveals-increased-personal-financial-Responsibility-among-americans-goals-save-more-reduce-debt

Chapter 8

Money And Wealth Quotes, http://www.behappy101.com/money-and-wealth-quotes.html
Cost Recovery, http://financial-dictionary.thefreedictionary.com/cost + recovery

How To: Set Up And Keep Financial Goals, http://www.moneymanagement.org/Budgeting-Tools/Credit-Articles/Money-and-Budgeting/How-To-Set-and-Keep-Personal-Financial-Goals.aspx

Market Crashes: The Dotcom Crash. http://www.investopedia.com/features/crashes/crashes8.asp

Economic Value Added (EVA): Its Uses And Limitations,

http://www.freepatentsonline.com/article/SAM-Advanced-Management-Journal/55015596.html

Shaked, Israel, Michel, Allen, Leroy, Pierre, *Creating Value Through EVA – Myth Or Reality?* http://www.strategy-business.com/article/12756?gko = 05fdd

Chapter 9

Money and Wealth Quotes,
http://www.behappy101.com/money-and-wealth-quotes.html

Clark, Kim, *What Is A Loan?*
http://www.usnews.com/education/best-colleges/paying-for-college/student-loan/articles/2010/10/08/what-is-a-loan

Cost Recovery, http://financial-dictionary.thefreedictionary.com/cost + recovery

Chapter 10

Money And Wealth Quotes,
http://www.behappy101.com/money-and-wealth-quotes.html

Kim Kiyosaki, What Is Financial Freedom?,
http://www.richdad.com/Resources/Rich-Dad-Financial-Education-Blog/January-2012/What-is-Financial-Freedom.aspx

Robert Laura, *These Retirement Stats Paint a Troubling Picture,*
http://www.fa-mag.com/news/these-retirement-stats-paints-a-troubleing-picture-16493.html

ABOUT THE AUTHORS

Raymond C. Poteet, Heather Graves, and Holly Reed all play vital roles at Living Wealth. Ray is the founder, Heather is the president, and Holly is the chief operating officer. Located in Lawrence, Kansas, Living Wealth was established in 1972 to sell life insurance and developed over the years to become a full service, financial planning and investment firm.

Living Wealth has since returned to where it started selling life insurance, only now we're selling life insurance as a tool to bring financial peace to families using the PFF and GPS processes. Today, we service both the average individual and some of the top small business leaders from a variety of professions. Much of the success of Living Wealth is due to the keen financial insight that Ray, Heather, and Holly have developed.

Raymond C. Poteet must be considered a success in the financial arena, not because of the money he has made for himself, but because of the dreams he has helped his clients achieve. Using his concepts and financial products, he has provided countless homes for families, numerous college educations for children, much better retirement living, and more wealth passed to survivors for their continuing lives. It is virtually impossible to explain how much good his financial insights and counseling have done.

Ray is a committed Christian and lives his life to the glory of God and his personal savior, Jesus Christ. Ray feels strongly that all his actions and those of his company are consistent with his spiritual beliefs. Ray has received numerous accreditations and honors. Among the many he has received; the following stand out in the financial industry:

- Chartered Financial Consultant
- Chartered Life Underwriter
- Life and Qualifying Member of the Million Dollar Round Table
- National leader in developing banks for small business and individuals through Infinite Banking Concept (IBC)
- Top Performance Awards from numerous financial institutions for many years running

Heather Graves is the middle child of Ray and Imy Poteet's three children. Heather started her first banking policy in 2005, the same year she received her license in life, health, and accident insurance and joined the family business. Since then, Living Wealth has come to include seven family members.

Heather previously worked for a non-profit organization and attended Azusa Pacific University and received a Bachelor of Science in Psychology in 1996. Heather believes that Private Family Financing is a ministry that allows anyone to create a family legacy while breaking the bonds of financial slavery. This is not only a business to her and her family, but a ministry that touches each generation of a family.

Holly Reed is the youngest daughter of Ray and Imy Poteet and the identical twin of Heather Graves. Holly joined the Living Wealth team and family business in 2009 and started a banking policy the same year. Holly is thrilled to be educating and helping as many individuals and families as possible understand money, get out of debt, and find financial freedom.

Holly graduated from Azusa Pacific Universality in 2000 with a

Master's in Education and College Student Affairs. Holly's passion, determination, and dedication has grown to help everyone she can break the bonds of financial slavery using the Private Family Financing system. Holly is always happy and available to listen, advise, and help people reach their financial goals.